PRO TIP TOP ENGLISH

3e Prépa métiers

A2-B1

W0346493

F. Bascou, professeure d'anglais au lycée polyvalent Alfred Kastler, Talence (33)
J. Herter, professeure d'anglais au lycée des Métiers Émile Baudot, Wassy (52)
B. Léonori, professeure d'anglais honoraire
S. Ritter, IEN Anglais-Lettres, académie de Reims
É. Rumburg, professeure d'anglais au lycée professionnel Le Champ de Claye, Claye-Souilly (77)
B. Sirjean, professeure d'anglais au lycée des Métiers Marie Marvingt, Tomblaine (54)

FOUCHER

Sommaire

ISBN 978-2-216-16842-2

« Le Code de la Propriété Intellectuelle n'autorisant aux termes de l'article L. 122-5, d'une part, que, les copies ou reproductions strictement réservées à l'usage privé du copiste et non destinées à une utilisation collective et, d'autre part, que, les analyses et courtes citations dans un but notamment d'exemple et d'illustration, toute représentation ou reproduction intégrale ou partielle, faite, par quelque procédé que ce soit, sans le consentement de l'auteur, ou de ses ayants droit est illicite et constitue une contrefaçon sanctionnée par les articles L. 335-2 et suivants du Code de la Propriété Intellectuelle. Le Centre Français de l'exploitation de la Copie (20, rue des Grands-Augustins 75006 Paris) est, conformément à l'article L. 122-10, le seul habilité à délivrer des autorisations de reproduction par reprographie, sous réserve en cas d'utilisation aux fins de vente, de location, de publicité ou de promotion de l'accord de l'auteur ou des ayants droit. »

© Foucher, une marque des éditions Hatier – Paris, 2023.

"Le photocopillage, c'est l'usage abusif et collectif de la photocopie sans autorisation des auteurs et des éditeurs. Largement répandu dans les établissements d'enseignement, le photocopillage menace l'avenir du livre, car il met en danger son équilibre économique. Il prive les auteurs d'une juste rémunération. En dehors de l'usage privé du copiste, toute reproduction totale ou partielle de cet ouvrage est interdite".

DANGER
LE PHOTOCOPILLAGE TUE LE LIVRE

UNIT 5 Going Out p. 47

Grammaire
L'heure digitale, les dates, inviter quelqu'un, répondre à une invitation
Phonologie
Les nombres

UNIT 6 Team Sports p. 57

Grammaire
Exprimer l'obligation : *must* + BV, exprimer l'interdiction : *mustn't* + BV, exprimer une possibilité : *can* + BV
Phonologie
must et *mustn't*

Conception graphique Anne-Danielle Naname
Adaptation maquette et mise en page Bénédicte Chantalou, Yuruga
Iconographie Sophie Labrousse
Relecture Victoria Britten
Illustrations Sara Lomuscio

UNIT 1 Express Yourself

PROJECT A2

In order to get to know each other better, everyone in your class will produce a short video. Introduce yourself in less than a minute in a selfie video.

A

Hello, I'm Lily! I'm from Manchester. I'm a .... And here is my ...., Tino.

B

Hi! My .... is Henry. Here are my stepsister[1] Rosie and my .... Kate.

1 *demi-sœur*

C

Hi everybody! .... to the USA! My name is William and I .... New York.

1 01 **Look at the pictures and fill in the missing words. Then listen and check.**

girlfriend • parrot • 'm from • name • student • Welcome

2 **Answer the questions.**

a. Who is from New York? ....

b. Who has a parrot? ....

c. Who has a stepsister called Rosie? ....

UNIT 1 All about me!

ACTIVITY A Hello from Australia!

1:26
VIDÉO
Introducing Yourself | ESL Listening & Speaking
foucherconnect.fr/23pttpm13

1 Watch the video from the beginning to 0:59 and tick what you understand.

a. The video is about teenagers:
☐ describing ☐ introducing themselves.

b. Anna says: "I'm: ☐ 18 ☐ 19 and I'm from Queensland".

c. Amber says: "☐ G'day ☐ Good evening"

d. Paige says: "☐ Hi everybody! ☐ Good morning."

e. Jordan says: "My: ☐ nickname ☐ name is Jordan and I'm 15".

2 Watch the video from 1:00 to the end and fill in the missing words.

a. Jack says: "…………………. My …………………. is Jack. I'm ……………….."

b. Marie says: "Hi! ……………… Marie and I am 14 …………………. old. I ……………… in Cairns, Australia".

3 Answer Paige and introduce yourself (greeting, name, age, place of living).

ACTIVITY B Sharing personal information

1 (02) Listen and select the elements you hear.

Name	*(Ella / Leah)* Williamson	**Place of living**	*Boston / London*
Nationality	*Irish / English*	**Occupation**	Professional footballer for *(Arsenal / Tottenham)*
Age	*26 / 28*	**Family**	*a brother / a sister*
		Pets	*a cat / a dog*

2 (02) Listen again and complete the questions.

a. What's your …………………?

b. What ………………………. are you?

c. How ……………… are you?

d. ……………………. do you live?

e. What's your …………………………?

f. Do you have ………………….. and sisters?

3 Give any other details you have understood about this young woman.

GRAMMAR SPOT

a. My name is Jordan and I'm fifteen.

b. I am English. I have a brother.

➜ *Soulignez les formes conjuguées du verbe* be *(être).*

➜ *Que signifie le verbe* have *?* ………….

➜ *Pour indiquer son âge, on utilise :*
☐ *be* ☐ *have*

Training ex. 6 & 7 p. 12

ACTION 1

Poser des questions personnelles et y répondre

A2

Work in pairs. Go to p. 115 or 118 and imagine you are one of these famous personalities. Keep the name secret and answer your partner's questions to make him/her guess your name. Then swap roles.

What I like doing

ACTIVITY C Likes and dislikes

1 (03) Listen and write the activities Lucy likes or doesn't like.

2 (03) Listen again and fill the gaps with:

love • hate • like

"I .... video games. I .... running. And I .... waiting!"

Lucy

♥ 

a. ....

♥♥ 
b. ....

✗ 
c. ....

ACTIVITY D Enjoy your weekend!

1 Underline the verbs expressing likes and circle the ones expressing dislikes.

2 Find the English for:

a. *dessiner* (1): ....

b. *faire la vaisselle* (1): ....

c. *sortir* (2): ....

d. *se lever tôt* (2): ....

e. *nettoyer* (3): ....

3 Choose one of the comments and say in French what you have understood.

What do you like doing at weekends?

1. Daniel

I like playing rugby with my friends. I enjoy drawing and taking photos. I love cooking but I don't like washing up.

2. Anya

I love going out with my friends. I'm fond of playing football with my family. I hate getting up early; I prefer sleeping.

3. Sam

I really enjoy playing the guitar. I also like doing sports. I don't like cleaning my hamster's cage but I love playing with him. He's so funny!

GRAMMAR SPOT

a. I <u>like</u> video games.

b. I <u>enjoy</u> playing the guitar.

➡ *Les verbes soulignés permettent de parler de :*

☐ *ses habitudes*

☐ *ses goûts, ses préférences*

➡ *Ils peuvent être suivis :*

☐ *d'un nom*

☐ *d'un verbe. Entourez la terminaison de ce verbe.*

Training ex. 9, 10 & 11 p. 12

LET'S GO FURTHER!!!

Watch the video and take notes. Then explain what they like and don't like doing.

1:17

VIDÉO
What do you like doing?

foucherconnect.fr/23pttpm18

ACTION 2

A1+ **Rédiger un commentaire pour indiquer ce que l'on aime faire**

Just like Daniel, Anya and Sam in Activity D, write your own comment on what you like and don't like doing at weekends.

UNIT 1

Talented teenagers

ACTIVITY E

Sharing videos on Instagram

1 ANNA R.

415 posts · 3,346 followers · 289 following

Anna Riberly
– 15, Brighton
– Year 9, Patcham High School
– disabled
– Jamie ♥
– love ♫
– play the guitar and sing
Enjoy every minute of your life!
Here are links to listen to my songs and sing with me

2 LUJAKE

592 posts · 6,832 followers · 321 following

Lucas Jake
– 16, Edinburgh
– Year 10, Royal High School
– Bubble, my goldfish
– play rugby, speak Italian
– love having fun
– create comic videos
Follow me! You can watch my comic videos and laugh with me!
@lujaketeam

1 Fill in the labels with:

link to follow the Instagrammer • number of documents published • age • place of living • Instagrammer name • school year

2 Read the profiles and answer the questions.

a. Who can play the guitar and sing? ....
b. Who can create comic videos? ....
c. Who is in a relationship with Jamie? ....
d. Who has a goldfish? ....

3 Find the English for:

a. *classe de* (1): ....
b. *handicapé* (1): ....
c. *des liens* (1): ....
d. *mon poisson rouge* (2): ....
e. *suivez-moi* (2): ....

GRAMMAR SPOT

a. She can play the guitar.
b. He can play the piano and the sax.
c. I can't walk.

➔ can *se traduit souvent par :*
☐ *devoir* ☐ *pouvoir, savoir*

➔ can *est toujours suivi :*
☐ *d'un nom* ☐ *d'un verbe*

➔ *La forme négative de* can *est* .... *ou* cannot

Training ex. 8 p. 12

4 (04) Listen and complete what Anna says to introduce herself.

a. Hi! My .... is Anna. I'm 15 years .... and I'm in Year 9 at Patcham ....
b. I am .... I can't walk but I .... move around in my wheelchair.
c. I love music. I can .... the guitar and I .... singing.
d. Jamie is my .... He is a .... too. He can play the piano and the sax.
e. Jamie and I like .... new songs and we love sharing them with our ....

ACTION 3

A2 **Présenter le profil et les talents d'un Instagrammeur**

Imagine you are Lucas Jake. Use Profile 2 to introduce yourself (name, age, place of residence, school year, occupation, pet animal, hobbies and talents).

AUDIO foucherconnect.fr/23pttpm17

in TUNE

A 05 Écoutez et entourez les mots que vous entendez.

a. I / hi   b. is / his   c. eight / hate   d. as / has   e. you /who

B 06 Écoutez puis répétez en prononçant bien le /h/ (aspiré).

a. Hi! My name is Henry.
b. Hello! Who are you?
c. Have a nice day!
d. I hate hamsters.
e. Here is my high school.
f. How old are you?

1 Complétez les adjectifs de nationalité sous chaque drapeau.

Ireland

a. IR _ _ _

England

b. EN _ _ _ _ _

Great Britain

c. BR _ _ _ _ _

USA

d. AM_ _ _ _ _ _

France

e. FR_ _ _ _

2 Associez les expressions anglaises à leurs équivalents français.

a. Hello! Welcome! •
b. Here is my ... •
c. Hi everybody •
d. Good morning •
e. I'm from ... •
f. Good evening •

• 1. *Bonjour*
• 2. *Salut tout le monde*
• 3. *Bonsoir*
• 4. *Salut! Bienvenue!*
• 5. *Je suis de ...*
• 6. *Voici mon/ma ...*

3 Complétez les mots manquants.

a. Hello! My .... is Benjamin and my nickname .... Benji.
b. I'm fourteen .... old and I'm .... Great Britain.
c. I .... in Winchester, England.
d. I study at Millbrook High .... and I'm in .... 9.
e. I have a cat .... Simba.

4 Rayez l'intrus dans chaque liste de mots.

a. sing – play the piano – listen to rap music – play golf – play the sax
b. use the phone – write a postcard – watch series – text – surf the Net
c. cycle – run – read – go horse-riding – play baseball
d. a sister – a boyfriend – a stepbrother – a cat – a baby
e. name – hello – age – nationality – place of living

5 Challenge!

Vous avez 2 minutes pour donner le plus grand nombre possible de loisirs.

Training

6 **Complétez avec *be* conjugué au présent.**

a. Lucas .... an Instagrammer.

b. We .... students in a vocational high school.

c. I .... a musician.

d. .... Jack American?

e. .... you from New York?

7 **Complétez avec *be* ou *have* conjugué.**

a. I .... a dog called Cooper.

b. I .... 16 years old.

c. My nickname .... Betty.

d. He .... a new scooter.

8 **Ajoutez *can* ou *can't* selon ce que vous savez faire ou non.**

a. I .... speak two foreign languages.

b. I .... swim.

c. I .... play football.

d. I .... play the guitar.

e. I .... draw very well.

9 **Soulignez la ou les traductions qui conviennent.**

a. like: *adorer – aimer – détester*

b. love: *adorer – préférer – aimer une personne*

c. hate: *détester – haïr – apprécier*

d. enjoy: *préférer – aimer – apprécier*

e. prefer: *avoir horreur de – préférer – aimer mieux*

10 07 **Complétez avec les verbes à la forme qui convient. Puis écoutez et vérifiez.**

play • create • sing • read • watch

a. I enjoy .... music videos.

b. They love .... video games.

c. My brother likes .... fiction books.

d. You hate .... very old songs.

e. I don't like .... comic videos.

11 **Rédigez 3 énoncés pour parler de vos goûts ou de vos loisirs. Utilisez *like, love, enjoy*.**

a. ....

b. ....

c. ....

TIPS — LANGUAGE

Be au présent

Be s'utilise pour exprimer un état.

Forme affirmative

I am/'m – he/she/it is/'s – we/you/they are/'re

I am a student. *Je suis étudiant.*

Forme négative

I am not/I'm not – he/she/it is not/isn't – we/you/they are not/aren't

She isn't Irish. *Elle n'est pas irlandaise*

Forme interrogative

Am I...? – Is he/she/it ...? – Are we/you/they ...?

Are they from London? *Sont-ils de Londres ?*

! On utilise *be* pour indiquer l'âge.
He is 18 (years old). *Il a 18 ans.*

Have

Have s'utilise pour exprimer la possession.

I have/'ve – he/she has/'s – we/you/they have/'ve

She has two brothers. *Elle a deux frères.*

L'expression des goûts

Les verbes comme like, love, enjoy, prefer, hate s'utilisent pour dire ce que l'on aime ou pas.
Ils peuvent être suivis d'un nom ou d'un verbe en *-ing* (BV + *-ing*).

I love music. *J'adore la musique.*

I enjoy reading mangas. *J'aime lire des mangas.*

Can / can't

Ils s'utilisent pour exprimer ce que l'on sait/peut faire ou pas. can / can't + BV

He can sing. *Il sait/peut chanter.*

They can't move. *Ils ne peuvent pas bouger.*

Word Page

AUDIO
foucherconnect.fr/23pttpm34

Sport *Le sport*

run*
courir

ride* a bike/cycle
faire du vélo

play basketball
jouer au basket

swim*
nager

Music *La musique*

listen to music
écouter de la musique

sing*
chanter

play the guitar
jouer de la guitare

play the sax
jouer du saxo

Leisure *Les loisirs*

watch series
regarder des séries

read*
lire

take* photos
prendre des photos

draw*
dessiner

play video games
jouer aux jeux vidéo

phone
téléphoner

text
envoyer des textos

surf the Net
surfer sur Internet

Pet Animals *Les animaux de compagnie*

a dog
un chien

a cat
un chat

a parrot
un perroquet

a goldfish
un poisson rouge

Vocabulary

Nouns

a boy/girlfriend *un(e) petit(e) ami(e)*
a brother *un frère*
a half/step brother/sister *un(e) demi-frère/sœur*
a musician *un(e) musicien(ne)*
a name *un nom*
a nickname *un surnom*
a sister *une sœur*
a song *une chanson*
a student *un(e) étudiant(e)*
a wheelchair *un fauteuil roulant*

Verbs

clean *nettoyer*
create *créer*
follow *suivre*
go* out *sortir*
have* fun *s'amuser*
introduce myself/yourself *me/te présenter*
laugh *rire*
live *vivre, habiter*
share *partager*
speak* *parler*
walk *marcher*
wash up *faire la vaisselle*

UNIT 1

PROJECT

A2

Introduce yourself

in a short video

SCENARIO

Afin de mieux faire connaissance en ce début d'année, vous créez une vidéo selfie d'une minute pour vous présenter. Vous déposerez cette vidéo sur le mur virtuel de la classe.

A1+

Compléter une fiche de renseignements

- Complétez la fiche ci-dessous. Ajoutez d'autres informations en bas de la fiche si vous le souhaitez.

→ First name: ....

→ Age .... Nationality ....

→ Place of residence ....

→ (Step- / Half-) Brothers / Sisters ....

....

→ Friends ....

....

→ Pets ....

→ School .... Year ....

→ Likes and dislikes ....

....

→ Hobbies and talents ....

....

→ Favourite social network ....

→ Other ....

....

....

....

A2

Créer une vidéo pour se présenter

- Utilisez les éléments de votre fiche pour vous présenter à l'oral.
- Entraînez-vous à parler distinctement et à bien prononcer. Vous pouvez vous connecter à un site de prononciation pour vous aider, comme www.naturalreaders.com ou www.fromtexttospeech.com.
- Procédez à l'enregistrement vidéo. Recommencez plusieurs fois si nécessaire.
- Déposez votre vidéo sur le mur virtuel de la classe.

CULTURE CLICK 1 COMIC BOOK SUPERHEROES

1 Look at the picture and name the superheroes you know.

2 Write the aliases in the labels: Ant-Man • Captain America • Iron Man • Hulk

3 08 Listen to the presentation of these heroes and tick the right answers.

	Iron Man	Ant-Man	Captain America
Occupation: He is ...	a rich: ☐ builder ☐ engineer	☐ an ex-thief ☐ an ex-criminal	☐ a soldier ☐ a teacher
Abilities: He can ...	☐ become invisible ☐ fly ☐ break walls	☐ communicate with insects ☐ swim ☐ shrink in size	☐ talk to animals ☐ run very fast ☐ lift heavy things
Accessories: He has ...	☐ armour ☐ a lasso ☐ high-tech weapons	☐ a crown ☐ a helmet	☐ a shield ☐ a sword
He first appeared in ...	☐ December 1952 ☐ December 1962	☐ January 1962 ☐ February 1962	☐ March 1941 ☐ May 1941

CULTURE CLICK 1 COMIC BOOK SUPERHEROES

QUIZ

1. Stan Lee was:
- ☐ a. an American actor
- ☐ b. a comic book writer
- ☐ c. a superhero

2. Which superhero was invented to fight in WWII?
- ☐ a. The Hulk
- ☐ b. Captain America
- ☐ c. Thor

3. What insect bit Peter Parker and gave him his powers?
- ☐ a. a bat
- ☐ b. a spider
- ☐ c. a fly

4. Which superhero can manipulate the weather?
- ☐ a. The Flash
- ☐ b. Storm
- ☐ c. Electro

5. Which superhero gets his power from a ring?
- ☐ a. Green Hornet
- ☐ b. Magneto
- ☐ c. Green Lantern

6. Wolverine is a member of:
- ☐ a. the Justice League
- ☐ b. the Avengers
- ☐ c. the X-Men

7. The Fantastic Four are: the Invisible Woman, the Thing, Mister Fantastic and ...
- ☐ a. Mister Freeze
- ☐ b. the Human Torch
- ☐ c. Storm

8. Batman lives in:
- ☐ a. New York City
- ☐ b. Gotham City
- ☐ c. Starling City

9. The first Spider-Man comic was:
- ☐ a. *Amazing Fantasy #15*
- ☐ b. *The Amazing Spider-Man #1*
- ☐ c. *Spider-Man #1*

10. The name of Thor's new hammer is:
- ☐ a. Stormdestroyer
- ☐ b. Stormbuilder
- ☐ c. Stormbreaker

11 **Listen and check.**

Your score: ..../10

Did You Know Why Superheroes Are So Popular?

The golden age of American superhero comics began in 1938, when DC Comics introduced Superman as the first costumed crime fighter in *Action Comics #1*. [...] Batman entered the scene in 1939, and Wonder Woman, Captain Marvel, and the Human Torch were not far behind. [...] When World War II broke out in 1939, comic books reacted: in 1941 Captain America made his first appearance on a Marvel Comics cover, punching Adolf Hitler. With new issues released biweekly or monthly, superhero comics were able to include timely to current events. Their attention to the American civil rights movement, feminism, wars, and political scandals [...] garnered[1] an audience of devoted fans that would follow the adventures of their favorite heroes for decades.

1. *recueillir*

www.britannica.com.

4 Read the document and answer the questions.

a. When did Superman first appear? ....

b. How did comic books react when WWII broke out?

....

....

c. What events were mentioned in the comics? ....

....

....

5 09 **Listen and underline the correct information.**

The Most Popular Female Comic Book Superhero

For over (*60* / *80*) years, Wonder Woman has proven that a superheroine can be just as (*popular* / *famous*) as her (*friend* / *male*) superheroes. First appearing in (*1931* / *1941*), Wonder Woman quickly became one of DC Comics' (*funniest* / *greatest*) heroes. Like every other superhero, Wonder Woman has a (*private* / *secret*) identity. She is Diana Prince and comes from Paradise Island, home of the (*amazing* / *legendary*) Amazons. Like her fellow heroes' (*suits* / *outfits*), Wonder Woman's costume has evolved over time.

6 10 **Listen and match the descriptions of her costume to the corresponding pictures.**

Description	a	b	c
Picture n°	.....	.....	.....

You can watch a video to see the evolution of Wonder Woman's costume.

2:12
VIDÉO
Wonder woman Transformation Movie
foucherconnect.fr/23pttpm28

UNIT 2 Job Exploration

PROJECT A2+

To help everyone discover jobs, your class will post job descriptions on the class virtual wall. Make and post one of these descriptions.

B. Job: Barista / Fast food team member
Tasks: She prepares food and ...., ... customers and keeps the restaurant clean.

A. Job: Security Agent / Firefighter
Tasks: They .... the safety of people, objects or .... in person or via security cameras.

C. Job: Electrician / Plumber
Tasks: He installs, maintains and .... pipes and .... systems.

1 **Look at the pictures and underline the corresponding jobs.**

2 (12) **Listen and fill in the blanks with:**

ensure • repairs • serves • plumbing • buildings • drinks

3 (13) **Fill in the corresponding jobs. Then listen and check.**

a. A .... extinguishes fires, rescues and protects people.
b. An .... installs, maintains and repairs electrical systems.
c. A .... prepares and serves hot and cold drinks.

Job overview

ACTIVITY A Where do you work?

1 (14) **Match the sentences. Then listen and check.**

a. "I'm a cashier." • • 1. "I work in a garage"

b. "I work as a car mechanic." • • 2. "I work in a tailor's shop."

c. "We are nursing assistants." • • 3. "I work in a supermarket."

d. "I work as a dressmaker" • • 4. "We work in a hospital."

2 (15) **Fill in the job titles. Then listen and check.**

a. A .... scans products and takes payments.

b. A .... makes, repairs and alters clothing for men, women and children.

c. A .... is responsible for inspecting and repairing vehicles.

d. .... care for patients, serve meals and assist doctors and nurses.

ACTIVITY B What does your job consist of?

(16) **Match the questions with Tina's answers. Then listen and complete her answers.**

a. What's your job? (....)
b. Where do you work? (....)
c. What does your job consist of? (....)
d. What do you like about your job? (....)

1. I enjoy working in a team. I love .... and .... furniture.
2. I'm a joiner[1].
3. I work in a .... workshop[2].
4. I make and .... doors, ... and furniture.

1 *un menuisier* 2 *un atelier*

GRAMMAR SPOT

a. Where do you work?
I work in a large workshop.

b. What does your job consist of? I make and repair doors.

➜ *L'ordre des mots dans ces questions au présent simple est :*

.... + do/does + ... + *base verbale* + ?

➜ *Les verbes conjugués au présent simple expriment :* ☐ *une vérité générale* ☐ *un souhait* ☐ *une habitude*

c. I'm a joiner.

➜ *Traduisez cet énoncé. Que remarquez-vous devant le nom de métier ?*

....
....
....

Training ex. 8 & 9 p. 22

ACTION 1

Poser et répondre à des questions sur un métier (A2)

Work in pairs. Student A: go to p. 116. Student B: go to p. 119. Use the information to ask and answer questions about the jobs.

Job profiles

VIDÉO
Teens Jobs
by Edward Green
foucherconnect.fr/23pttpm08

ACTIVITY C Teen jobs

1 Watch the video and number the different parts in the order you see them.

...... The jobs teenagers have ...... The periods when teenagers work ...... How many hours they can work

2 Watch again and tick true or false. Justify orally when false.

a. 14- and 15-year-old teenagers don't work during the school year. True ☐ False ☐

b. In the US, teens can only work 18 hours a week during the holidays. True ☐ False ☐

c. They cannot work after 7 PM. True ☐ False ☐

3 Complete with the jobs mentioned in the video.

a. She serves at table in a restaurant. She is ....

b. She watches and looks after children when their parents are absent. She is ....

c. He takes care of your garden. He is ....

ACTIVITY D My job as a bakery assistant

1 (17) Listen and complete.

Ryan has a NVQ[1] certificate in sales. He works as an .... in a bakery shop. He sells ...., cakes, pastries, salads and .... He advises and .... He also keeps the shop .... He likes his job. He thinks he has a good salary. But he has .... days and he doesn't like finishing .... late.

1 National Vocational Qualification *(équivalent CAP)*

2 Answer the questions orally.

a. What is Ryan's qualification?

b. What does he sell?

c. What are the positive and negative aspects of his job?

GRAMMAR SPOT

a. **I <u>work</u> in a supermarket.**

b. **She <u>watches</u> and <u>looks</u> after children.**

➜ *À la forme affirmative du présent simple, on ajoute « -s » ou « -es » au verbe :* ☐ *à la 1re personne* ☐ *à la 3e personne du singulier*

c. **Teenagers <u>don't work</u> during the school year.**

d. **He <u>doesn't like</u> finishing work late.**

➜ *À la forme négative, l'ordre des mots est : Sujet + ... + ... (+ complément)*

Training ex. 5, 6 & 7 p. 22

LET'S GO FURTHER!!!

Watch the video and explain what you have understood about Kim's job and the reasons why she loves it.

VIDÉO
The Overnight Baker
1:58
foucherconnect.fr/23pttpm09

ACTION 2

Rédiger un paragraphe pour faire deviner un métier

A2+

Work in pairs. Choose a job mentioned in the unit and keep it secret. Write a paragraph to present it. Your partner will have to guess the name of the job.

© Éditions Foucher

A job description

ACTIVITY E

Bus driver

1 ....

....

Average salary (a year)
£18.000 — £34.000
Starter → Experienced

Typical hours (a week)
45 to 47
variable

You could work
evenings
weekends
bank holidays
away from home

2 ....

Bus drivers are required[1] to drive buses in order to transport passengers from one place to another. They are responsible for the safety and comfort of their clients while they travel on the bus. [...]

3 ....

- Checking transport passes
- Helping passengers with difficulties to get on and off
- Driving legally and safely
- Monitoring vehicle parts [...]

4 ....

- Having excellent driving skills
- Having good knowledge about routes and geography
- Being polite and assertive [...]
- Being able to work under pressure
- Having knowledge about safety and health issues
- Being responsible and reliable [...]

5 ....

Every job placement involving[2] bus driving requires a special licence, so bus driver applicants need to have a PCV licence[3] for this purpose.

1 sont tenus 2 impliquant 3 un permis pour transporter des passagers

www.jobisjob.co.uk.

1 **Give each section one of the subtitles below.**

Qualifications • Working conditions • Tasks • Description • Skills

2 **Circle the right translation.**

a. an average salary (1): *un salaire minimum / un salaire moyen*
b. travel (2): *s'asseoir / voyager*
c. get on and off (3): *monter et descendre / aller et venir*
d. work under pressure (4): *vérifier la pression des pneus / travailler sous pression*
e. health issues (4): *issues de secours / problèmes de santé*

3 **Answer the questions.**

a. How many hours a week do bus drivers work?

....

b. What does their job consist of?

....

c. Do they need good communication skills?

....

....

d. What is the qualification they need?

....

4 **Say if you would like to be a bus driver and give your opinion about the job.**

WORD BOX

- **an applicant** un candidat
- **assertive** sûr de soi
- **check** vérifier
- **knowledge** des connaissances
- **monitor** surveiller
- **reliable** fiable
- **safety** la sécurité
- **a skill** une compétence

ACTION 3

MÉDIATION A2+

Rendre compte d'une fiche métier

Say in French what you have understood about the document.

© Éditions Foucher

Training

AUDIO
foucherconnect.fr/23pttpm07

In TUNE

A 18 **Écoutez et répétez ces verbes conjugués au présent simple.**

/s/ She works   /z/ He sells   /iz/ She watches

B 19 **Écoutez et cochez selon la prononciation.**

	He takes	She manages	He feeds	It does	She creates	He organises	She likes
/s/	☐	☐	☐	☐	☐	☐	☐
/z/	☐	☐	☐	☐	☐	☐	☐
/iz/	☐	☐	☐	☐	☐	☐	☐

1 Complétez les noms des lieux de travail sous chaque image.

a. G........................

b. B........................

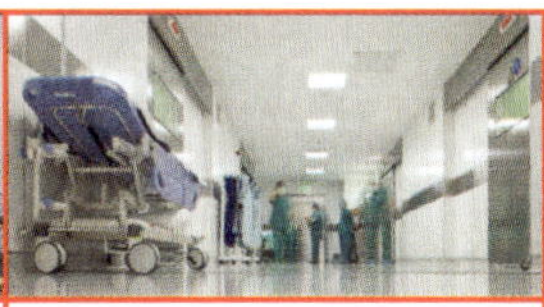
c. H........................

d. W........................

e. T............s..........

2 Reliez chaque métier à ses tâches possibles.

a. baby-sitter •
b. joiner •
c. bus driver •
d. shop assistant •
e. nursing assistant •
f. car mechanic •

• 1. inspecting and repairing vehicles
• 2. looking after children
• 3. making and repairing furniture
• 4. driving safely and checking transport passes
• 5. advising and serving customers
• 6. caring for patients

3 Complétez les phrases avec les verbes.

scan • maintain • serve • install • care for

a. Waiters and waitresses take orders and .... at table in a restaurant.
b. Doctors, nurses and nursing assistants .... patients in a hospital.
c. Supermarket cashiers .... products and take payments.
d. Gardeners cut grass and .... parks and gardens.
e. Electricians .... and repair electrical systems.

4 Challenge!

Vous avez 2 minutes pour donner le plus grand nombre possible de noms de métiers.

Training

5 **Réécrivez ces phrases à la 3e personne du singulier (« he » ou « she »).**

a. I work as a taxi driver. ....

....

b. They watch the dogs. ....

c. We don't like working under pressure. ....

....

d. Do you work in a tailor's shop? ....

....

6 **Conjuguez les verbes entre parenthèses au présent simple.**

a. I .... and .... plumbing systems. *(install / repair)*

b. He .... the tables clean and .... the dishes. *(keep / wash)*

c. Bus drivers .... transport passes and .... passengers when necessary. *(check / help)*

d. Our company .... and .... gardens and parks. *(design / manage)*

7 **Conjuguez les verbes à la forme négative du présent simple.**

a. I .... long working days. *(like)*

b. She .... to finish work late. *(want)*

c. They .... a good salary. *(get)*

d. We .... working in an office. *(enjoy)*

e. A baby-sitter .... animals. *(take care of)*

8 **Entourez la forme verbale qui convient.**

a. *(Do / Does)* you work in a restaurant?
b. What *(do / does)* your job consist of?
c. What *(do / does)* the waiters like about their jobs?
d. When *(do / does)* your service finish?

9 **Complétez les questions.**

a. Where ....
▶ I work in a bakery shop.

b. When ....
▶ She starts work on Monday.

c. What ....
▶ They prefer working from home.

TIPS — LANGUAGE

Le présent simple

Il s'utilise pour exprimer des actions habituelles ou des vérités générales.

Forme affirmative

- ***I / you / we / they*** **+ BV**
- ***He / she / it*** **+ BV + -*s*** (ou ***-es*** pour les verbes se terminant par –o, -ch, -sh, -s, -x et –z).

I repair cars. *Je répare des voitures.*

She watches the children. *Elle veille sur les enfants.*

Forme négative

Sujet + *don't/doesn't* + BV

I don't work in a shop. *Je ne travaille pas dans un magasin.*

He doesn't like working late. *Il n'aime pas travailler tard.*

Forme interrogative

L'ordre des mots dans une question est:

(Pronom interrogatif) + *do/does* + sujet + BV + (complément) +?

Do you drive a bus? *Conduis-tu un bus?*

Where does he work? *Où travaille-t-il?*

⚠ Si *Who* est sujet du verbe: ***Who*** **+ BV + -*s* (+ complément) +?**

Who works as a florist? *Qui travaille comme fleuriste?*

UNIT 2

Word Page

AUDIO
foucherconnect.fr/23pttpm35

Jobs *Les métiers*

a shop assistant
un(e) vendeur(se)

a cashier
un(e) caissier(ère)

a waiter/waitress
un(e) serveur(se)

a nursing assistant
un(e) aide-soignant(e)

an electrician
un(e) éléctricien(ne)

a plumber
un(e) plombier(ère)

a joiner
un(e) menuisier(ère)

a gardener
un(e) jardinier(ère)

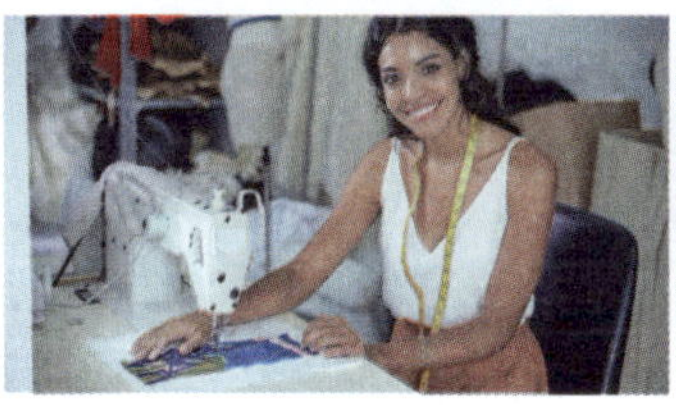

a dressmaker
un(e) couturier(ère)

a bus driver
un(e) chauffeur de bus

a florist
un(e) fleuriste

a delivery boy/girl
un(e) livreur(se)

Tasks *Les tâches*

repair
réparer

maintain
assurer l'entretien de

check
vérifier, contrôler

clean
nettoyer

serve
servir

take* payments
encaisser

deliver
livrer

feed*
nourrir

Vocabulary

Nouns

a bakery *une boulangerie*
a firefighter *un pompier*
a qualification *un diplôme*
a salary *un salaire*
a skill *une compétence*
a task *une tâche*
a team member *un membre de l'équipe*
a workshop *un atelier*

Verbs

advise *conseiller*
be* responsible for *être responsable de*
care for *prendre soin de*
design *dessiner, concevoir*
install *installer*
look after *s'occuper de*
manage *gérer, diriger*
rescue *sauver*
scan *scanner*
sell* *vendre*
take* care of *s'occuper de, prendre soin de*
watch *surveiller*

Adjectives

clean *propre*
reliable *fiable*
useful *utile*

UNIT 2 A2+

PROJECT Create a job description

SCENARIO

Dans le cadre du Parcours Avenir et afin de vous aider à vous orienter vers une famille de métiers, votre classe va mettre en ligne des fiches métiers sur le mur collaboratif de la classe. Réalisez et postez une de ces fiches.

A2 MÉDIATION

Trouver les informations pertinentes

- Choisissez un métier qui vous intéresse.
- Trouvez les informations utiles pour compléter la fiche descriptive ci-dessous.
  Si besoin, vous pouvez vous aider des sites proposés:
  – https://nationalcareersservice.direct.gov.uk
  – https://www.prospects.ac.uk/job-profiles

→ Job: ....

→ Main tasks
- ....
- ....
- ....
- ....
- ....
- ....

→ Skills
- ....
- ....
- ....
- ....
- ....
- ....

→ Place(s) of work
- ....
- ....
- ....
- ....

→ Working conditions
- ....
- ....
- ....
- ....
- ....
- ....

→ British qualifications *(and their French equivalents)*:

☐ NVQ[1] ....
(CAP ....*)*

☐ BTEC[2] National Diploma ....
(Baccalauréat Professionnel ....
ou Brevet Professionnel ....*)*

☐ BTEC[2] Higher National diploma ....
(BTS ....*)*

1 National Vocational Qualification
2 Business and Technology Education Council

A2+

Créer une fiche métier

- Utilisez les éléments de votre fiche descriptive pour réaliser votre fiche métier.
  Rédigez plusieurs phrases par rubrique.
- Vous pouvez insérer des photos (professionnel au travail, lieu de travail, tenue, matériel...).
- Mettez en valeur ce qui vous paraît important. Soignez la présentation. Relisez bien.
- Mettez votre fiche métier en ligne.

Méthode 1
Comprendre un document sonore

1 Avant l'écoute

1 Anticipez le thème du document
Avant la première écoute ou le premier visionnage, utilisez le titre et/ou l'image pour émettre des hypothèses sur le contenu du document (thème, lexique...). Si le titre fait référence à un fait culturel, une période historique ou un personnage, réfléchissez à tout ce que vous savez à ce sujet et aux mots que vous pourriez entendre.

2 Observez la source du document: elle peut vous orienter sur sa nature (bulletin d'information, documentaire, extrait de film, publicité...).

2 Pendant l'écoute

3 Au cours de la 1re écoute ou du 1er visionnage, repérez: le nombre de locuteurs (combien de personnes parlent ?), le lieu de l'action et le thème général (quel est le sujet ?).

4 Au cours de la 2e écoute ou du 2e visionnage, repérez: les noms propres, les mots clés, les mots transparents, les indications chiffrées, les indices temporels, les informations importantes et éventuellement la structure du document.

5 Au cours de la 3e écoute ou du 3e visionnage, repérez: les informations secondaires et les détails.

3 Après la troisième écoute

6 Prenez du temps pour faire le point sur ce que vous avez compris et pour identifier les liens entre les éléments repérés.
Décidez des passages qu'il vous faut ré-écouter attentivement pour repérer les éléments marquants.

Entraînez-vous !

1 **Observez le titre de la vidéo et émettez des hypothèses sur le sujet du document.**

1:29
VIDÉO
Tips for Teens on Finding a Summer Job
foucherconnect.fr/23pttpm31

....

....

2 **Regardez une première fois la vidéo et cochez les bonnes réponses.**

a. The document is: ☐ an extract from a TV series ☐ a TV commercial ☐ a documentary ☐ a report

b. The document is presenting: ☐ one ☐ two ☐ three ☐ four teenagers.

c. The subject of the document is:
☐ teens' jobs ☐ teens' hobbies ☐ teens' addictions ☐ teens' favourite sports

3 **Regardez à nouveau le document une ou deux fois et complétez :**

a. Les noms propres : Gabe Heller – Angeli Budron – Gabe Jaffi

b. Les mots clés : ....

c. Les mots transparents : ....

d. Les indications chiffrées : ....

....

e. Les informations importantes sur les métiers : ....

....

....

4 **Regardez à nouveau le document et repérez les éléments suivants :**

Les informations secondaires et les détails : ....

....

5 **Rédigez un résumé de la vidéo.**

....

....

....

6 **Faites un résumé de cette vidéo en suivant la méthode de la page 25.**

1:24
VIDÉO
The Role of a YouTuber
foucherconnect.fr/23pttpm32

....

....

....

....

....

UNIT 3

Time for Shopping

PROJECT A2

You are on a work placement in a shopping mall. Act a dialogue with a customer.

1 **Look at the photos and tick the correct elements.**

a. The scene takes place at the information desk in:
☐ a shopping centre ☐ an airport

b. The mall is:
☐ closed ☐ open on Sundays.

c. The stores open at:
☐ 10 am ☐ 10 pm

2 20 **Listen and fill in the speech bubbles with:**

next to • floor • on • store

3 **Say where you like shopping, with who and when.**

Hello. On which .... is there a leather* ....?

*cuir

There's one .... the second floor, ... the sports shop.

UNIT 3

Shopping for groceries

ACTIVITY A At the grocery store

1 Tick the right element to complete the definition of a grocery.

A grocery is a store where customers can buy: ☐ food ☐ clothes

2 (21) Listen and fill in the speech bubbles.

3 Find the English equivalents in the speech bubbles.

a. *Comment ... ?:* ....

b. *Je cherche...:* ....

c. *Aimeriez-vous... ?:* ....

d. *du pain:* ....

e. *Voici pour vous:* ....

f. *De rien:* ....

GRAMMAR SPOT

- **Would you like** to buy white or brown bread?

Les mots soulignés se traduisent par: ☐ *Voulez-vous ... ?* ☐ *Aimeriez-vous... ?*

Training ex. 5 p. 32

ACTIVITY B Product labels

Write the words corresponding to the definitions and the number of the corresponding logos.

sugar-free • vegan • dairy-free • gluten-free

a. It doesn't contain milk from an animal:

.... logo N° .....

b. It doesn't contain sugar:

.... logo N° .....

c. It doesn't contain products derived from animals:

.... logo N° .....

d. It doesn't contain gluten:

.... logo N° .....

ACTION 1

A2 Demander et comprendre des informations pour un achat

Use Activity A to act a dialogue with your partner. You are buying one of these items: ice cream – biscuits – chewing gum – chocolate **with a characteristic from Activity B.**

At the mall

ACTIVITY C At the shoe shop

1 22 **Listen and tick the correct answers.**

a. The customer wants to buy a pair of: ☐ boots ☐ sneakers
b. He is size: ☐ 5 ☐ 6
c. He chooses: ☐ plain ☐ striped shoes.

2 22 **Listen again and complete. Then match with the French equivalents.**

a. What .... are you? •
b. Would you like to .... them ....? •
c. Do they ....? •
d. How .... are they? •
e. How are you ....? •

• 1. *Combien coûtent-elles ?*
• 2. *Quelle est votre pointure / taille ?*
• 3. *Comment payez-vous ?*
• 4. *Est-ce qu'elles vous vont ?*
• 5. *Voudriez-vous les essayer ?*

ACTIVITY D In a clothes store

Watch the video to 1'53" and say if the sentences are true or false.

a. The woman wants a new dress to go to a wedding*. T F
b. The first dress she tries on is too small. T F
c. The size 10 dress fits the woman. T F
d. The dress costs £150. T F
e. She pays by cheque. T F

* *mariage*

3:13
VIDÉO
It Suits You – In A Clothes Shop
foucherconnect.fr/23pttpm36

GRAMMAR SPOT

a. **$69.50 → sixty-nine dollars fifty**
b. **£150 → a hundred and fifty pounds**

En anglais, lorsqu'on écrit un prix, l'unité monétaire se place : ☐ *devant* ☐ *après* *le prix.*

Training ex. 3 p. 32

LET'S GO FURTHER!!!

Watch the video from 1'54" to the end and answer the questions.

a. What does the woman want the man to buy?
....
b. What size does he ask for?
....
c. Is the shirt expensive?
....
d. How much is the shirt?
....

ACTION 2

A2 **Simuler un sketch de vente**

DOCUMENT
foucherconnect.fr/23pttpm33

In pairs, use the elements to act a dialogue. One of you is the sales assistant, the other is the customer. Then swap roles.

UNIT 3

Customer feedback

ACTIVITY E

Poor quality clothes

https://www.xara.com/customerfeedback/

Jane C.
1 review • 3 helpful votes
★☆☆☆☆ July 10th, 2023

Horrible experience! Don't buy clothes from Xara website. I am not satisfied at all with the clothes they sell. The size is never right: they are always too long or too short. Another problem is the colours of the patterns[1]. The colours are often different from the photos on the website: sometimes they are too light and sometimes they are too dark. I ordered two dresses, a pair of black trousers and a tee-shirt on xara.com and they forgot to send me the trousers, without even refunding me! And when I tried to return the tee-shirt they didn't accept it, claiming a missing[2] price tag. Stupid customer service. I won't shop from Xara again! Please think about this before ordering.

1 *motifs* 2 *manquante*

1 Look at the top of the document and answer the questions.

a. What is the customer's name? ....

b. When did she post this message? ....

c. Is she satisfied? Justify. ....

2 Find the English equivalents.

a. *clair*: ....

b. *commander*: ....

c. *oublier de*: ....

d. *envoyer*: ....

e. *rembourser*: ....

f. *une étiquette de prix*: ....

3 Right or wrong? Justify with elements from the document.

a. The brand name[1] of the clothes Jane bought is Xara. R / W ....

b. Jane bought accessories. R / W ....

c. She is not satisfied with the sizes and the prices. R / W ....

d. She didn't like the tee-shirt she ordered. R / W ....

e. It was easy to return the tee-shirt. R / W ....

1 *marque*

GRAMMAR SPOT

a. They're too long or too short.

b. Black trousers.

Devant un adjectif, le mot « too » signifie :
☐ *trop* ☐ *aussi*

Traduisez l'item b. Que remarquez-vous ?

....

....

Training ex. 2 & 4 p. 31-32

ACTION 3

Rédiger un avis de consommateur A2

Write a post about your last customer experience on a website. Write about what you bought and say if you liked what you received or not.

UNIT 3

Training

AUDIO

foucherconnect.fr/23pttpm37

in TUNE

A 23 **Écoutez puis associez les mots comportant la même diphtongue.**

a. here /ɪə/ •	• 1. clothes
b. go /əʊ/ •	• 2. beer
c. how /aʊ/ •	• 3. size
d. sure /ʊə/ •	• 4. poor
e. grey /eɪ/ •	• 5. trousers
f. tight /aɪ/ •	• 6. trainers

B 24 **Écoutez, vérifiez puis répétez.**

1 **Classez les articles dans les rayons de grand magasin où l'on peut les trouver.**

lipstick  • saucepan  • camera  • salad  • ice cream  • yoghurt 
• shampoo  • milk  • apples  • French fries  • mug  • TV set 

Dairy	Frozen food	Fresh produce	Houseware	Cosmetics	Electronics
....	....	....	....	....	....
....	....	....	....	....	....

2 **Indiquez le nom de chaque vêtement avec l'article a/an (+ nom singulier) ou 0 (+ nom pluriel). Si besoin, utilisez un dictionnaire en ligne.**

1.	2.	3.	4.	5. ....

6.	7.	8.	9.	10. ....

11.	12.	13.	14.	15. ....

Training

3 (25) **Écoutez et associez les prix avec les articles.**

1. 
2. 
3. 
4. 

a. €15
b. $39.90
c. £54.99
d. $8

4 Complétez en écrivant ce qui ne convient pas.

a. The dress is ....

b. The shirt is ....

c. The tee-shirt is ....

d. The trousers are ....

5 (26) **Complétez le dialogue avec les répliques suivantes. Puis écoutez et vérifiez.**

Would you like to try these on? • How much are they? • I'd like to try these trousers on • Can I help you? • How are they?

Shop assistant: ....

Customer: Yes, please. Where are the fitting rooms?

....

Shop assistant: The fitting rooms? They're over there, next to the jackets.

Customer: Thanks.

Shop assistant: (*a few minutes later*)

....

Customer: They're a bit too tight.

Shop assistant: Just a minute.

....

Customer: Hmm, yes. I'll try them on.

Shop assistant: Do they fit all right?

Customer: Yes, they're fine.

....

Shop assistant: They're £39.

Customer: OK, I'll take them.

Shop assistant: Anything else?

Customer: No, thanks.

LANGUAGE TIPS

Faire une suggestion

Would you **like** white bread?
Aimeriez-vous du pain blanc ?

Yes, please / No, thank you.
Oui, merci / Non, merci.

Dire ce que l'on aimerait

He **would like** a pair of black trousers.
Il aimerait un pantalon noir.

I**'d like** a blue dress.
J'aimerais une robe bleue.

Dire et écrire des prix

£15 → fifteen pounds
quinze livres sterling

$110 → a/one hundred and ten dollars
cent dix dollars

€2.99 → two euros ninety-nine
deux euros quatre-vingt-dix-neuf

Too + adjectif

These trousers are **too** long.
Ce pantalon est trop long.

UNIT 3

Word Page

AUDIO
foucherconnect.fr/23pttpm38

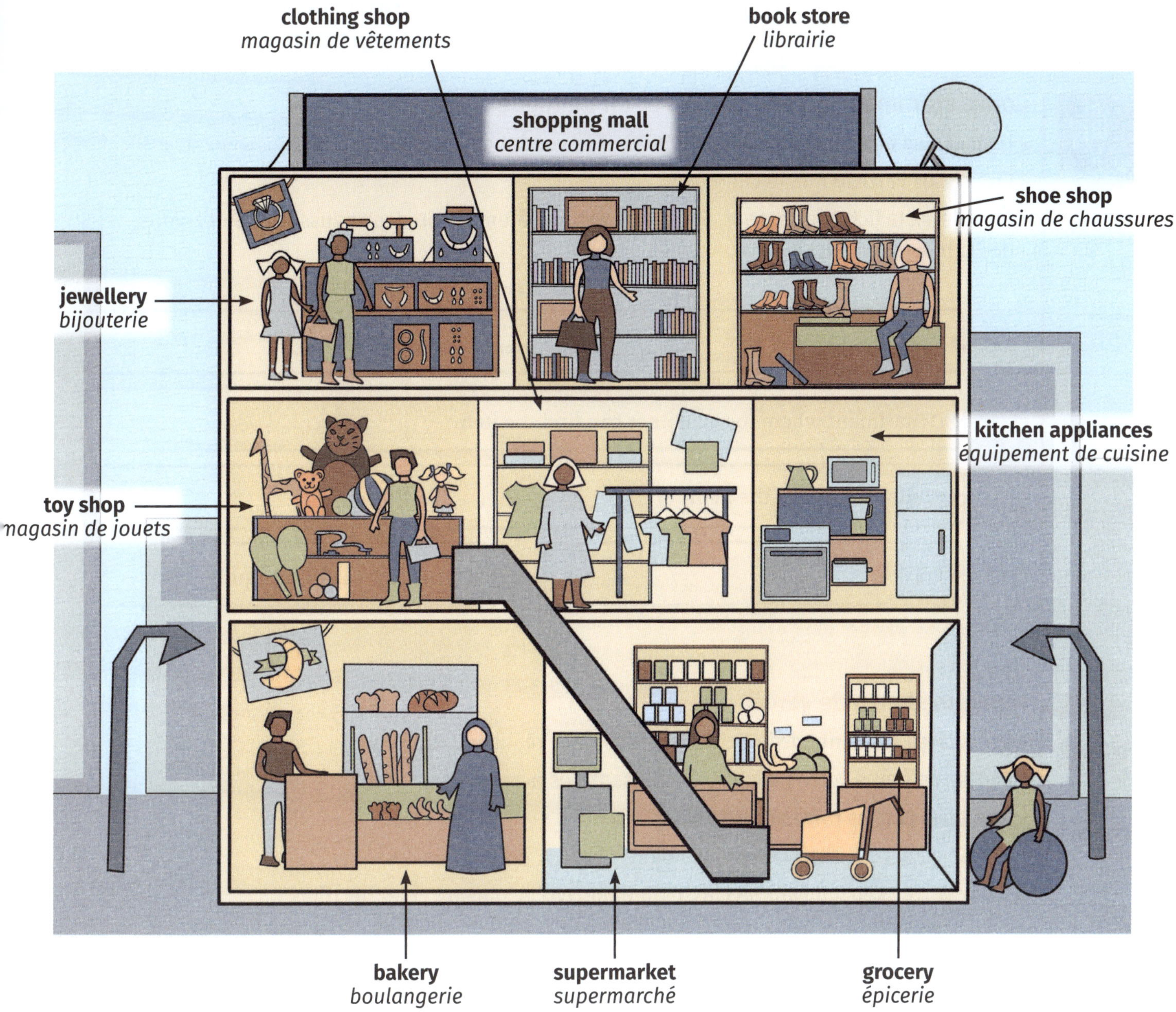

Vocabulary

Nouns

cash *des espèces*
a cheque *un chèque*
a bank/credit card *une carte bancaire/de crédit*
a customer *un client*
a grocery *une épicerie*
a mall *un centre commercial*
a price *un prix*
a shop/store *un magasin, une boutique*
a shop assistant *un vendeur*
a size *une taille*

Verbs

buy* *acheter*
fit *convenir, être de la bonne taille*
help *aider*
look for *chercher*
order *commander*
refund *rembourser*
return *retourner*
sell* *vendre*
try on *essayer*

Adjectives

cheap *pas cher, économique*
closed *fermé*
dark *foncé*
expensive *cher*
large *grand*
light *clair*
open *ouvert*
short *court*
tight *serré*

UNIT 3

PROJECT

A2

Act a dialogue in a shop

SCENARIO

Vous êtes en stage dans un centre commercial et un client arrive. Simulez le dialogue que vous avez avec lui.

A1

Compléter une fiche pour préparer un dialogue

- Formez des binômes : l'un d'entre vous est le vendeur, l'autre est le client.
- Choisissez l'article que le client veut acheter.
- Complétez la fiche ci-dessous. Si l'article est un vêtement ou des chaussures, aidez-vous des tableaux en bas de page.

→ Name of the item: ....

→ Department where the customer can find the item: ....

→ Characteristics of the item ....

→ Price: £........... / $........... / ....€

→ Payment: ☐ card ☐ cheque ☐ cash

A2

Jouer un sketch de vente

- Utilisez les éléments de la fiche ci-dessus pour réaliser votre sketch.
- Mettez en scène votre dialogue en utilisant des accessoires.
- N'oubliez pas les formules de politesse.
- Entraînez-vous à répéter votre dialogue.
- Jouez votre sketch devant la classe ou filmez-vous, puis inversez les rôles.

Euro	UK	USA	International
34	8	4	XS
36	10	6	S
38	12	8	M
40	14	10	L
42	16	12	XL
44	18	14	XXL
46	20	16	
48	22	18	

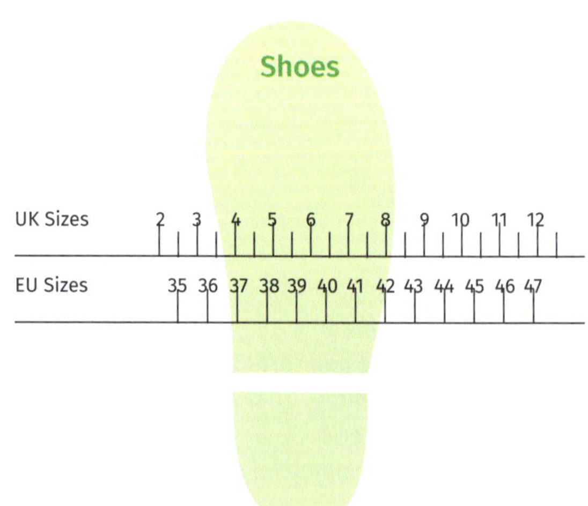

CULTURE CLICK 2 KING CHARLES III

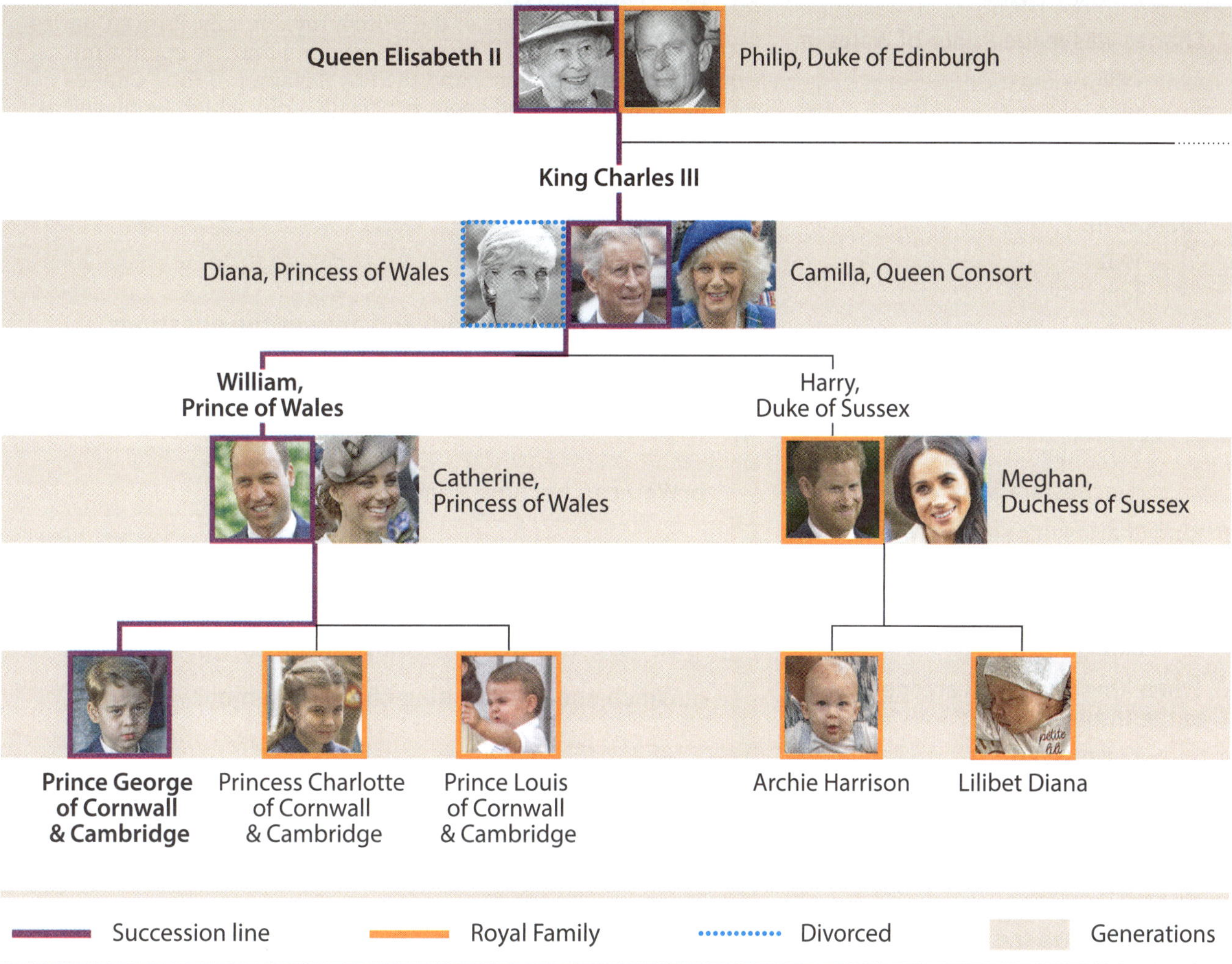

1 27 **Look at the family tree and tick the correct answers. Listen and check.**

a. King Charles III's father was: ☐ Philip, Duke of Edinburgh ☐ William, Duke of Cornwall and Cambridge
b. Queen Elizabeth II is King Charles III's: ☐ grandmother ☐ mother
c. Meghan, Duchess of Sussex, is King Charles III's: ☐ daughter ☐ daughter-in-law
d. Prince George is King Charles III's: ☐ son ☐ grandson
e. Camilla is King Charles III's: ☐ wife ☐ sister

2 **Answer the questions.**

a. Who will be sovereign after King Charles III? ....
b. How many grandchildren does King Charles III have? ....
c. Who is Prince Louis's uncle? ....
d. Who divorced King Charles III? ....
e. Who was Queen Elizabeth II's husband? ....

CULTURE CLICK 2 KING CHARLES III

QUIZ

1. King Charles III was born at:
- ☐ a. Clarence House
- ☐ b. Buckingham Palace
- ☐ c. Windsor Castle

2. Charles was made Prince of Wales in:
- ☐ a. 1958
- ☐ b. 1959
- ☐ c. 1960

3. Prince Charles married Lady Diana Spencer in:
- ☐ a. 1981
- ☐ b. 1984
- ☐ c. 1986

4. The place of his coronation was:
- ☐ a. St Paul's Cathedral
- ☐ b. Westminster Abbey
- ☐ c. Winchester Cathedral

5. King Charles III's second wife is:
- ☐ a. Alexandra
- ☐ b. Regina
- ☐ c. Camilla

6. When King Charles III acceded to the throne, he was:
- ☐ a. 73 years old
- ☐ b. 74 years old
- ☐ c. 75 years old

7. Since 2022, the British national anthem is:
- ☐ a. God Save the Queen
- ☐ b. God Save the King
- ☐ c. God Save the Prince

8. King Charles III's favourite sport is:
- ☐ a. football
- ☐ b. rugby
- ☐ c. polo

9. The person next in line to the throne is:
- ☐ a. Harry
- ☐ b. William
- ☐ c. George

10. King Charles III studied at:
- ☐ a. Cambridge University
- ☐ b. Oxford University
- ☐ c. York University

29 **Listen and check.**

Your score: ..../10

Charles Philip Arthur George was born at Buckingham Palace, London, on November 14, 1948. [...] In 1952, when Prince Charles was three years old, his mother became Queen Elizabeth II. From then on, Prince Charles became first in line to the British throne. He went to schools in London, Hampshire and Scotland and then attended the University of Cambridge. He earned a bachelor's degree[1] there in 1971. In 1958 Queen Elizabeth made Prince Charles the prince of Wales. This is an ancient title, traditionally given to the eldest son of the British monarch. [...] Like many members of the British royal family, Prince Charles served in the armed forces. As a young man he spent time in the Royal Air Force and the Royal Navy. [...] King Charles has always enjoyed sport, especially polo, which he played as a young man. He likes skiing, fishing, and painting, and he is interested in architecture, the countryside and organic[2] farming.

https://kids.britannica.com.

1. *licence* 2. *biologique*

3 Read the document and answer the questions.

a. Does King Charles III have a diploma?

....

b. Who can become Prince of Wales?

....

c. Is King Charles III the only member of the royal family to have served in the Army? ....

d. Which sports does King Charles III enjoy?

....

e. Does he like nature?

....

....

4 28 **Listen and circle the items which change when a new king or queen accedes to the throne in the UK.**

UNIT 4 A House for Reality TV

PROJECT A2

You are taking part in a contest to design the setting for a reality TV programme. Imagine the perfect accommodation for the candidates and describe it.

INCREDIBLE PROPERTIES FOR INCREDIBLE EVENTS

A

Type: ....

Advantages: .... & ....

B

Type: ....

Advantages: .... & ....

C

Type: ....

Advantages: .... & ....

D

Type: ....

Advantages: .... & ....

1 30 **Fill in the labels with the different types of accommodation. Listen and check.**

a farmhouse • a castle • a villa • an eco-house

2 30 **Listen again and write the corresponding adjectives.**

traditional • quiet • beautiful • comfortable • natural • luxurious • modern • lovely

3 **Say which type of accommodation you prefer and why.**

UNIT 4

Inside the house

ACTIVITY A

The Simpsons' house

1 **Look at the plans below and say if the sentences are true (T) or false (F).**

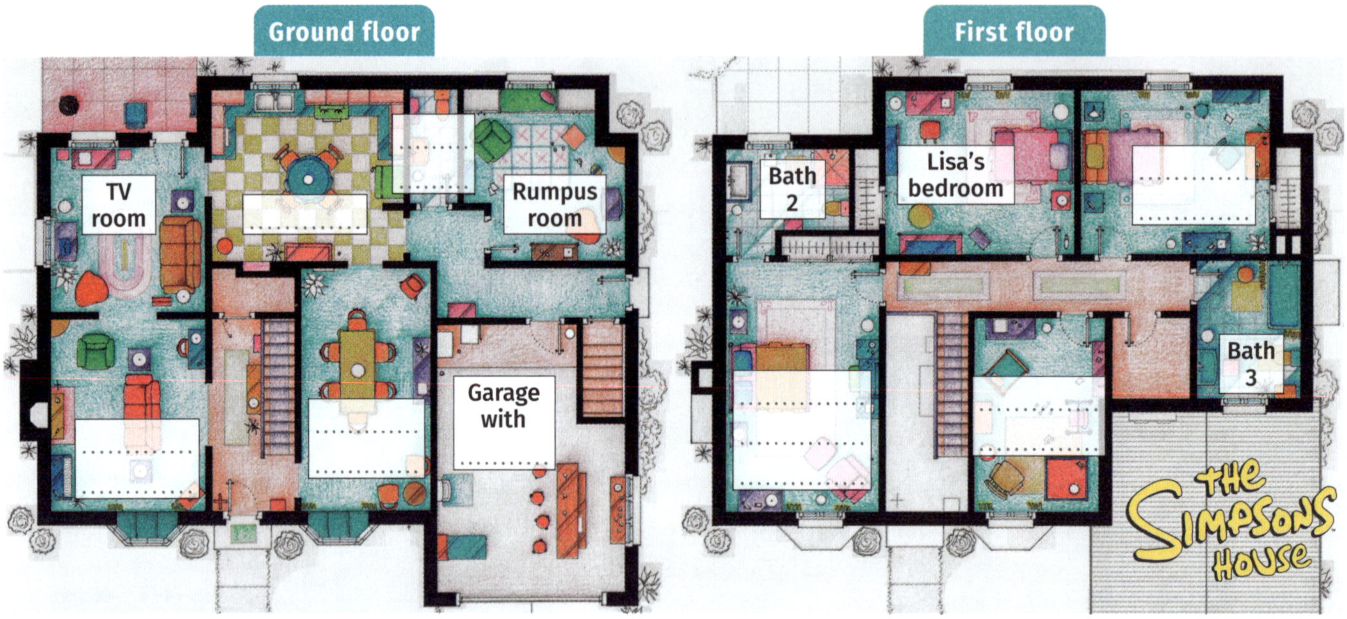

a. The Simpsons' house is made up of two floors. T F
b. There are eight rooms and a garage on the ground floor. T F
c. The garage is between the rumpus room and the TV room. T F
d. There is no bathroom on the ground floor. T F
e. There are six rooms on the first floor. T F
f. There is a terrace. T F

2 69 **Listen and write the names of the missing rooms.**

WORD BOX

- **between** entre
- **a corridor** un couloir
- **a floor** un étage, un sol
- **next to** à côté de
- **opposite** en face de
- **a rumpus room** une salle de jeux

GRAMMAR SPOT

a. There is a long corridor.
b. There are six rooms.

Les éléments soulignés se traduisent par ....

« There is » *est immédiatement suivi d'un groupe nominal au :* ☐ *singulier* ☐ *pluriel*

« There are » *est immédiatement suivi d'un groupe nominal au :* ☐ *singulier* ☐ *pluriel*

Training ex. 5 & 7 p. 42

ACTION 1

Décrire l'agencement des pièces d'une maison

A1+

Student A: go on p. 117. Look at plan A and describe it so that your partner can complete his/her document. Then swap roles: your partner describes plan B on p. 122 and you complete your document.

Home decoration

ACTIVITY B — An amazing interior for Big Brother

.....

.....

.....

1 (audio 31) **Listen and match the descriptions with the corresponding pictures.**

2 (audio 31) **Listen again and tick what you hear.**

a. The bedroom has several: ☐ single beds ☐ double beds
There is no: ☐ door ☐ window and there are red: ☐ curtains ☐ chairs

b. The bathroom has: ☐ yellow ☐ golden furniture.
There are several: ☐ mirrors ☐ showers and a large: ☐ rug ☐ bath

c. In the living-room, there are: ☐ red ☐ blue couches with many cushions.
The walls and the floor have a: ☐ geometric ☐ floral design.

GRAMMAR SPOT

- **The bedroom has several beautiful beds.**

➜ *Soulignez l'adjectif. Où est-il placé ?*

....

➜ *Que remarquez-vous ?* ....

Training ex. 6 p. 42

WORD BOX

- **a couch** un canapé
- **curtains** des rideaux
- **a cushion** un coussin
- **furniture** le mobilier
- **a rug** un tapis
- **a wall** un mur

ACTIVITY C — A sea atmosphere

Match the descriptions (a-b) with the pictures. Then fill in the labels with the words in bold letters.

a. In this bedroom, there is a large **coral sculpture** surrounded by four double beds. There is also a **chair** and a **wardrobe**. On the walls, blue panels reproduce the sea.

b. This bedroom has big ship's masts[1] above the three **double beds**. There is also a couch and a large **cabinet** in the room.

1 *mâts de navire*

.....

.....

ACTION 2

A2

Décrire des pièces à partir d'images

Describe one of the rooms on p. 115.

UNIT 4

Outside the house

ACTIVITY D Harry Potter's school

1 Read the text and circle True (T) or False (F).

	T	F
a. Harry Potter's school is a castle.	T	F
b. Hogwarts is in the USA.	T	F
c. The students can play sports.	T	F
d. Hagrid lives in the castle.	T	F

Hogwarts Castle is located in Scotland. It is surrounded by mountains and overlooks a lake. There is a wide lawn opposite the castle, flowerbeds, several greenhouses and a Quidditch pitch. There are pumpkin and vegetable patches in a garden next to Hagrid's hut, which is between the castle and the forest.

2 Find the equivalents in the text.

a. *une pelouse*: ....

b. *des serres*: ....

c. *un jardin*: ....

d. *des carrés de légumes*: ....

e. *un terrain (de sport)*: ....

f. *des parterres de fleurs*: ....

ACTIVITY E The Love Island villa

WORD BOX

- **outdoor** extérieur
- **overlook** surplomber
- **surrounded by** entouré par

1 32 **Listen and select what you hear.**

a. *Love Island* is a reality show broadcast on (*NBC* / *ITV*).

b. The show takes place in a big (*apartment* / *villa*) in Majorca, with a vast outdoor space to (*relax* / *sunbathe*) in.

c. There are (*sun loungers* / *day beds*) and rabbit chairs in the wonderful garden.

d. There are beautiful (*plants* / *trees*) growing along a pergola.

e. There is an outdoor (*bar* / *kitchen*), a fire pit and a (*swimming pool* / *hot tub*).

2 Write the corresponding words from exercise 1 under the pictures.

a. ....

b. ....

c. ....

d. ....

LET'S GO FURTHER!!!

Watch the video and describe the house.

1:01

VIDÉO
Inside a Prestigious Custom Built Home

foucherconnect.fr/23pttpm01

ACTION 3

A2

Rédiger une description d'un extérieur de propriété

Choose one of the places on p. 118 and describe it.

UNIT 4 # TRAINING

AUDIO foucherconnect.fr/23pttpm04

In TUNE

A 33 **Écoutez et répétez les mots.**

/θ/ think   /ð/ there

B 34 **Écoutez et cochez selon la prononciation.**

	a	b	c	d	e	f	g	h
/θ/	☐	☐	☐	☐	☐	☐	☐	☐
/ð/	☐	☐	☐	☐	☐	☐	☐	☐

1 Trouvez les lettres manquantes de ces pièces.

a. G _ R _ _ E
b. B _ _ R _ _ M
c. _ I _ _ _ E N
d. _ A T _ _ _ O M
e. L I _ _ _ G R _ _ _
f. _ U M _ _ S _ _ O M
g. D _ N _ _ _ _ O O _

2 Décrivez l'appartement de Joey et Chandler de la série *Friends* en complétant les phrases avec *next to*, *between* ou *opposite*.

a. The living room is .... the dining room and the bedrooms.
b. The front door is .... the kitchen.
c. Joey's bedroom is .... Chandler's bedroom.
d. The front door is .... the television.
e. The television is .... the armchairs.
f. There are cabinets .... the beds.

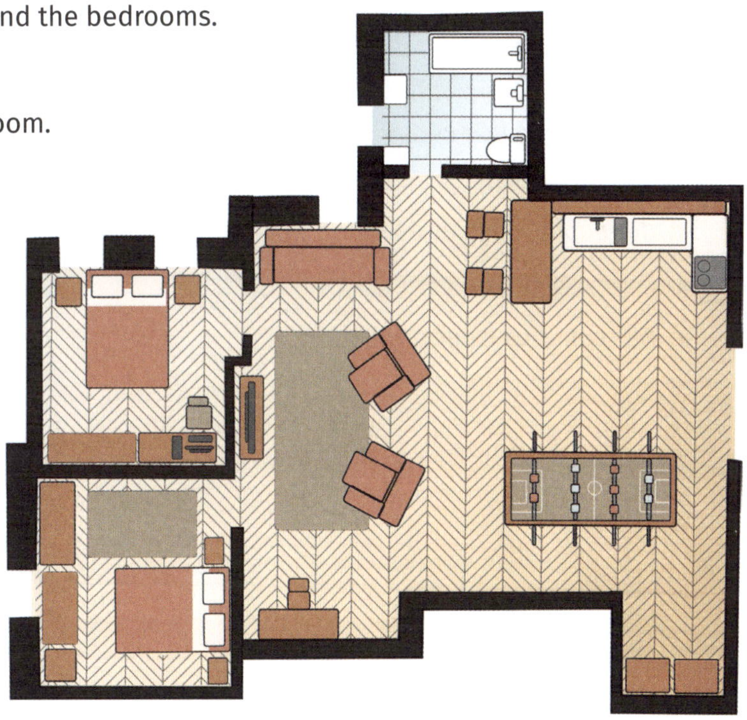

3 Complétez la description du même appartement avec les mots ci-dessous.

rug • chairs • bath • apartment • ground floor

a. Joey and Chandler live in an ....
b. They don't live on the ...., but on the third floor.
c. There is a large .... in the living room.
d. There are two .... in the kitchen.
e. There is a .... in the bathroom.

Challenge!

4 Vous avez deux minutes pour lister autant d'objets présents dans une maison que possible.

5 **Complétez avec *there is* ou *there are* à la forme qui convient (affirmative, négative ou interrogative).**

a. How many rooms .... in your apartment?
b. .... six rooms.
c. .... a bath?
d. Yes, ... And .... also a shower.
e. .... a balcony?
f. No, ...

6 **Traduisez les éléments ci-dessous.**

a. *une cuisine moderne*:
....
b. *des chaises noires et blanches*:
....
c. *des rideaux roses*:
....
d. *du mobilier luxueux*:
....
e. *des canapés confortables*:
....

7 **Traduisez les phrases suivantes.**

a. *Il y a un canapé bleu en face de la porte.*
....
b. *Il y a des plantes et des arbres à côté de la piscine.*
....
....
c. *Il y a des tapis jaunes entre les lits.*
....
d. *Il y a un beau jardin.*
....
e. *Il y a des chaises en forme de chaussure.*
....

8 **Complétez avec *be* ou *have* conjugués à la forme affirmative, puis traduisez oralement ces phrases.**

a. My house .... five rooms and a garage.
b. The bedrooms .... on the first floor.
c. The kitchen .... next to the hall.
d. The beds .... double beds.
e. The couch .... green and yellow cushions.
f. The bathroom .... a bath and a shower.

LANGUAGE TIPS

There is / There are

Pour traduire « il y a »

- **There is + singulier**
  There is a bath. *Il y a une baignoire.*
- **There are + pluriel**
  There are rugs. *Il y a des tapis.*

Pour demander « Y a-t-il ... ? »

- **Is there + singulier**
  Is there a garden? *Y a-t-il un jardin ?*
  → Yes, there is / No, there isn't.
- **Are there + pluriel**
  Are there sun loungers? *Y a-t-il des transats ?*
  → Yes, there are / No, there aren't.

Les adjectifs

En anglais, les adjectifs se placent **avant** les noms qu'ils qualifient et ils sont **invariables**.

There is an incredible garden. *Il y a un jardin incroyable.*

The walls are white. *Les murs sont blancs.*

UNIT 4

Word Page

AUDIO
foucherconnect.fr/23pttpm05

Parts of a house *Les parties d'une maison*

Objects and decoration *Objets et décoration*

an armchair *un fauteuil*

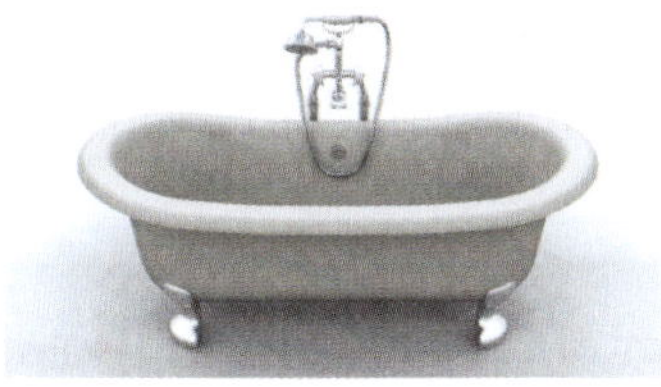
a bath *une baignoire*

a bed *un lit*

a cabinet *un petit meuble*

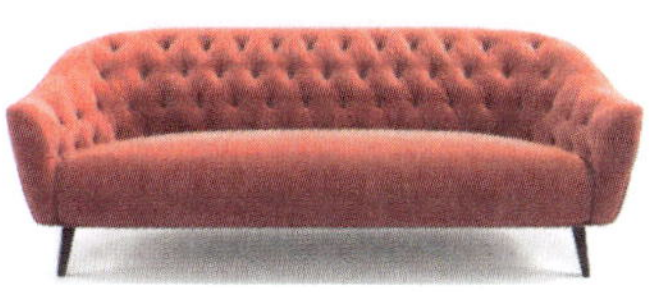
a couch *un canapé*

curtains *des rideaux*

cushions *des coussins*

furniture *le mobilier/des meubles*

a mirror *un miroir*

a rug *un tapis*

a shower *une douche*

a wardrobe *une armoire*

Vocabulary

Adjectives

beautiful *beau, belle*
comfortable *confortable*
lovely *adorable, charmant*
luxurious *luxueux*
modern *moderne*
natural *naturel*
quiet *tranquille*
traditional *traditionnel*

Types of accommodation

a castle *un château*
an eco-house *une maison écologique*
a farmhouse *une ferme*
a villa *une villa*

UNIT 4

A2

PROJECT — Imagine the perfect place

for the candidates of a TV reality programme

SCENARIO

Vous participez à un concours de création d'une habitation destinée aux candidats d'une émission de télé-réalité. Imaginez l'endroit idéal pour les candidats puis décrivez-le.

A1

Écrire des mots et expressions pour décrire l'extérieur d'une propriété

- Imaginez l'extérieur de la maison.

→ Type of accommodation:	→ Location:	→ Surrounding landscape:	→ Exterior/garden:
....	....	....	....
....	....	....	....

A1

Écrire des mots et expressions pour décrire l'intérieur d'une propriété

- Imaginez l'intérieur de la maison. Vous pouvez regarder la bande annonce de l'émission *Amazing Interiors* pour vous donner des idées.

VIDÉO foucherconnect.fr/23pttpm06

→ Number of floors: ....

→ Number of rooms: ....

→ Rooms: ....
....
....

Description of the rooms

→ Room 1
Theme/atmosphere: ....
Objects/decoration: ....
....

→ Room 2
Theme/atmosphere: ....
Objects/decoration: ....
....

→ Room 3
Theme/atmosphere: ....
Objects/decoration: ....
....

A2

Décrire une propriété

- Dessinez le plan de votre maison à la main ou avec un logiciel comme KoziKaza ou Sketch Up.
- Décrivez votre habitation grâce aux tableaux ci-dessus.
Commencez par l'extérieur, puis décrivez l'intérieur pièce par pièce.

MÉTHODE 2

Comprendre un document écrit

1 Avant de lire : anticipez sur le document et son contenu

1 **Identifiez la nature du document grâce à sa forme ou à sa source.** Il peut s'agir d'un article de journal, d'une BD, de paroles de chansons, d'un poème, d'un courrier électronique, d'un extrait de blog, etc.

2 **Émettez des hypothèses sur le thème du document.** Regardez les éventuelles illustrations et leurs légendes. Lisez le titre, les sous-titres, la date de publication. Imaginez le contenu du document.

2 Pendant la lecture : faites du repérage et appuyez-vous sur vos connaissances

3 **Vérifiez vos hypothèses en lisant le document et en repérant :**
- **les mots transparents** (qui ressemblent au français);
- **les indications chiffrées** (nombres, dates, prix, âges, horaires...);
- **les noms propres** (qui commencent par une majuscule afin d'identifier les lieux, les personnages, les marques, etc.).

4 **Repérez les temps principaux de chaque paragraphe et les marqueurs de temps** afin de voir si les informations sont passées, présentes ou futures.

5 **Repérez les mots clés, les mots qui sont répétés plusieurs fois, les champs lexicaux.**

6 **Repérez s'il y a des dialogues, des commentaires personnels...** grâce aux indices visuels comme les guillemets, l'italique.

7 **Repérez l'idée principale des différents paragraphes.**

8 **Déduisez le sens des mots inconnus** grâce au contexte, à leur composition (préfixes, suffixes...).

3 Lors d'une dernière lecture : faites des liens et accédez au sens global du document

9 **Essayez maintenant de répondre aux questions :** qui, quoi, où, quand, comment, pourquoi ?

10 **Cherchez les points de vue, les opinions mentionnés** dans le document et interrogez-vous sur **les intentions** de l'auteur.

11 **Mettez tous les éléments repérés en relation pour accéder au sens du document.**

Entraînez-vous !

Merle the eco mermaid swims non-stop for 12 hours to break record

By Sanj Atwal, published 09 June 2022

To spread awareness of the damage us humans are causing to our oceans, Merle Liivand (Estonia) decided to break her own record for the farthest swim with a monofin[1]. Wearing a mermaid[2] – like fin – and without using her arms – Merle swam 42.2 km (26.22 miles) around the coast of Miami Beach, Florida, USA on 7 May 2022. Her *fin-tastic* record attempt lasted for 11 hours 54 minutes! [...]

Merle first broke this record in April 2021, after swimming 30 km (18.6 miles) using her monofin. However, Merle knew she could do better. Over the next 13 months, Merle trained a lot harder and focussed on improving her breathing and nutrition. [...]

During the record attempt, Merle drank smoothies, baby food and soup whilst floating along. "You can't really eat anything heavy because you use your core[3] a lot," she said. Even though Merle was attempting to break a record, she didn't forget her eco mermaid responsibilities. She collected any plastic waste she found along the way and put it into the kayak rowing alongside. By the end of her swim, Merle had picked up enough plastic to fill three big bags!

1 *monopalme* 2 *sirène* 3 *ici : le centre de son corps*

https://kids.guinnessworldrecords.com.

1 **Observez le document et dites ce que vous savez sur :**

– le titre : ……………………………………………

……………………………………………

– la source : ……………………………………………

– l'image : ……………………………………………

……………………………………………

2 **À votre avis, de quoi va parler le document ?**

……………………………………………

3 **Lisez le texte et entourez les mots transparents. Puis trouvez les indications chiffrées qui correspondent à ces informations.**

a. …………………… = date du premier record

b. …………………… = distance parcourue à la nage en monopalme lors du premier record

c. …………………… = durée de l'entraînement entre les 2 records

d. …………………… = date du second record

e. …………………… = durée du second record de natation en monopalme

f. …………………… = distance parcourue à la nage en monopalme lors du second record

Enfin, repérez les noms propres.

– Personnage principal = ……………………

– Lieux = ……………………………………

4 **Repérez si les actions sont passées, présentes ou futures.** ……………………

5 **Identifiez les mots clés, les mots répétés.**

……………………………………………

6 **Soulignez les paroles prononcées, et identifiez l'auteur de ces paroles.** ……………………

7 **Donnez un titre à chaque paragraphe.**

……………………………………………

8 **Déduisez le sens des mots inconnus à partir du contexte.**

9 **Suivez maintenant les étapes 9 à 11 (page 45) pour rédiger un compte rendu du document.**

© Éditions Foucher

UNIT 5 Going Out

PROJECT A2

Act a dialogue to invite a friend to do an activity with you.

A

....

B

....

C

a day at ....

1 Write the words under the corresponding picture.

a. a theme park / a funfair b. a comics festival c. a concert

2 Complete with the following words.

see • have fun • sing • attractions • fans • superhero

a. When you go to a concert, you can .... songs with other ....

b. You can go to a comics festival if you want to .... your favourite ....

c. If you want to .... with your friends on new ...., go to a theme park.

3 Do you often go out with your friends? What do you like doing?

UNIT 5

Events

ACTIVITY A

Let's have fun!

1 35 **Listen and tick the correct information.**

Date: ☐ on Saturday 5th ☐ on Saturday 25th
Time: ☐ 4 PM ☐ 5 AM ☐ 5 PM
Price: ☐ £15 ☐ £20 ☐ £25 ☐ free[1]
Place: ☐ in town ☐ at the stadium

1 *gratuit*

Date: ☐ on 7th June ☐ on 6th June
Time: ☐ 2.15 AM ☐ 2.15 PM ☐ 3.15 PM
Price: ☐ £10 ☐ £15 ☐ free
Place: at the school: ☐ stadium ☐ gymnasium

2 **Complete the sentences with the information from exercise 1.**

a. There is a Fortnite .... on .... It starts at ....
It takes place .... It costs ....

b. There is an ....
on .... at ....
It takes place ....
.... It's ....

3 **Orally present the following events (date, time, price, place).**

Time: 9 pm
Price: £70

GRAMMAR SPOT

a. **4.15 AM** b. **7.30 PM**

➜ *Dites ces horaires à haute voix.*

➜ *Pour donner l'heure (digitale), on lit les nombres l'un .... l'autre.*

➜ *On utilise :*
☐ *AM/am* ☐ *PM/pm pour le matin*
☐ *AM/am* ☐ *PM/pm pour l'après-midi ou le soir.*

c. **Sunday 22nd** d. **December 6th**

➜ *En anglais britannique (UK), on dit :*
On Sunday the: ☐ twenty-two ☐ twenty-second
On the: ☐ six ☐ sixth of December

Training ex. 1, 3, 4 & 6 p. 51-52

ACTION 1

Annoncer un événement A1+

Student A: Go on p. 120 and present the event to your partner orally.
Student B: Listen to your partner and fill in the chart on p. 127. Then swap roles.

Invitations

ACTIVITY B Are you free?

1 36 **Listen to the conversation and answer the questions.**

a. Who is calling? ....

b. Who is invited? ....

c. Who is having a party? ....

d. What type of party is it? ....

e. What is the theme? ....

f. When is the party? ....

2 36 **Listen again and fill in the missing parts.**

a. "................ you .... next ....?"

b. "Would you .... to .... with me?"

c. "........................ is the party?"

d. "What about .... at 7.30 at the ....?"

GRAMMAR SPOT

a. **<u>Would you like to</u> come?**

b. **<u>What about</u> meeting at 7.30 PM?**

➔ *Les expressions soulignées servent à :* ☐ *conseiller* ☐ *inviter, proposer*

➔ Would you like to *est suivi d'une* ....

➔ What about *est suivi d'un verbe* ....

Training ex. 5, 7 & 8 p. 52

ACTIVITY C Great idea!

1 37 **Listen to the phone conversations and fill in the table.**

Conversation	Number	Number	Number .....
Who is invited?	....	....	....
What is the answer?	☐ Yes, that sounds good! ☐ No, I'm sorry, I hate science fiction movies. I prefer comedies.	☐ Yes, I'd love to. ☐ Sorry, but that's no fun.	☐ Yes, it's a great idea! ☐ No, thanks, I'm busy. I'm doing my homework.

2 **Find the English equivalents.**

a. *J'aimerais vraiment* ....

b. *Oui, ça a l'air bien !*

....

c. *Oui, c'est une idée géniale !*

....

d. *Désolé(e), ce n'est pas drôle*

....

e. *Non merci, je suis occupé(e)*

....

f. *Non, je suis désolée, je déteste...*

....

ACTION 2

Accepter ou refuser une invitation A2

Go on p. 121. Use the elements to act dialogues with your partner.
Student A: Invite him/her to come with you.
Student B: Answer the invitations. Agree (+) or refuse (-). Then swap roles.

© Éditions Foucher

UNIT 5

A day at Disneyland

ACTIVITY D Enjoy your visit!

1 Read the document and answer the questions.

a. What is the document about? ....

b. What can you do at Marvel Avengers Campus? ....

c. What kind of objects can you see at Bistrot chez Rémy? ....

Things to Do at Disneyland® Paris

If you're a Disney fan, you'll want to make sure you get the most out of your visit. That's why we've put together a handy guide of the things you MUST do during your visit.

- **Visit Marvel Avengers Campus:** Here you join your favourite heroes, including Black Widow, Captain Marvel, Thor and Captain America. There are two incredible new rides, [...] and exciting character encounters [...].
- **Watch the incredible stage show:** Disneyland® Paris has a number of live stage shows that will make you feel like you're sitting in a Broadway theatre!
- **Eat at Bistrot chez Rémy:** This restaurant is inspired by the Disney Pixar classic, *Ratatouille*. Everything inside is supersized. [...] There are giant umbrellas, plates, cookbooks and cutlery[1] all around the restaurant.

1 *des couverts*

www.attractiontickets.com.

2 Find the English equivalents.

a. *profiter au maximum de* (§1): ....

b. *un guide pratique* (§1): ....

c. *des nouveaux manèges* (§2): ....

d. *passionnante* (§2): ....

e. *des spectacles en direct* (§3): ....

f. *de très grande taille* (§4): ....

ACTIVITY E Planning a visit

To: JENNY <jenny.doll@gmail.com>
Subject: Disneyland Paris

Hi Jenny,
Only a week until you arrive! I'm preparing your visit! I know you love theme parks! So, would you like to go to Disneyland? We could spend the day there next Friday?
I want to organize the visit, so please, answer as soon as possible.
Angela xxx

To: ANGELA <angela.fun@gmail.com>
Subject: Disneyland Paris

Hi Angela,
Thanks a lot for the invitation. It sounds great! I'm crazy about theme parks! Of course I'd love to spend the whole day there with you.
Can't wait! Tell me what you plan to do.
See you next week.
Jenny xxx

Read the emails and answer the questions.

a. What does Angela suggest to Jenny? ....

b. When does she want to go? ....

c. Does Jenny accept the invitation? Why? ....

ACTION 3 A2

Répondre à un courriel

You are Angela. Use the document in Activity E to answer Jenny's email.

© Éditions Foucher

Training

AUDIO
foucherconnect.fr/23pttpm39

in TUNE

A 38 **Écoutez et répétez.** 1st - 2nd - 3rd - 5th - 9th - 20th - 21st - 30th

B 39 **Écoutez et entourez les nombres que vous entendez.**

a. 4 - 4th - 40 - 14 b. 3 - 3rd - 30 - 30th c. 20 - 20th - 21st - 23rd

1 **Retrouvez les 7 jours de la semaine cachés dans la grille. Notez-les ensuite dans l'ordre.**

B	T	W	P	D	C	N	S	Y
T	H	U	R	S	D	A	Y	A
U	S	X	U	U	T	I	V	D
R	U	D	G	U	H	F	M	N
W	N	T	R	Z	Y	O	U	O
S	D	D	H	S	U	M	Q	M
Y	A	D	S	E	N	D	E	W
Y	Y	F	R	I	D	A	Y	Z
K	Y	A	D	S	E	U	T	X

1. ....
2. ....
3. ....
4. ....
5. ....
6. ....
7. ....

2 **Reliez chaque activité à un lieu où l'on peut la pratiquer.**

a. Play tennis •
b. Listen to your favourite singer •
c. Run •
d. See Marvel characters •
e. Dance and have fun •
f. Have a picnic •

• 1. in a marathon
• 2. at a comics festival
• 3. in the park
• 4. at a party
• 5. at a concert
• 6. in the gym

3 **Écrivez ces horaires en toutes lettres en utilisant AM et PM.**

4:20
a. ....

14:30
b. ....

9:45
c. ....

21:15
d. ....

2:50
e. ....

17:00
f. ....

4 40 **Écoutez et complétez avec les horaires en chiffres.**

a. The party starts at ....
b. We could meet at ....
c. The football match is at ....
d. What about meeting at ....?
e. The concert is at ....
f. The show starts at ....

5 **Remettez les éléments dans l'ordre.**

a. to London / Would / go / to / you / like /? ....

b. I'd / Yes, / to / love / ! ....

c. about / the British Museum / What / visiting / ? ....

d. a great / Yes, / idea / that's / ! ....

6 **Dites oralement à quelles dates ont lieu ces événements.**

a. 

b. 

c. 

d. 

7 **Complétez en ajoutant le verbe à la forme qui convient.**

a. What about .... a picnic at the park? (*have*)

b. Would you like to .... to the swimming pool? (*go*)

c. What about .... football this afternoon? (*play*)

d. Would you like to .... a series? (*watch*)

8 **Complétez les dialogues en vous aidant des images.**

a.  ? 

b.  ? 

c.  ? 

a. – Would ....? → – Yes, ...

b. – What ....? → – No, ...

c. – Would ....? → – No, ...

LANGUAGE TIPS

L'heure digitale

Pour donner l'heure digitale, on lit simplement les nombres du cadran, dans l'ordre.
On précise **AM/am** pour le matin et **PM/pm** pour l'après-midi ou le soir.

9:00 AM → nine o'clock in the morning
2:15 PM → two fifteen in the afternoon
8:30 PM → eight thirty in the evening

Les dates (jour précis)

Pour dire ou écrire une date, on utilise les nombres ordinaux (1st, 2nd, 3rd, 4th…).

– On écrit: 14th May (UK); March 7th (US).

– On dit: **on** the fourteenth of May (UK); **on** March the seventh (US).

Inviter quelqu'un (à sortir, à faire une activité)

Would you like to + BV

Would you like to **go** to the cinema?
Aimerais-tu aller au cinéma?

What about + BV-*ing*

What about **going** to the cinema?
Et si on allait au cinéma?

Répondre à une invitation

Pour accepter

Yes, I'd love to. / Yes, that's a great idea. / Yes, that sounds good. *J'aimerais vraiment / C'est une idée géniale! / Oui, ça a l'air bien!*

Pour refuser

No, it's no fun / No, thanks, I'm busy / No, I'm sorry, I hate... *Non, ce n'est pas drôle / Non, merci, je suis occupé(e) / Non, désolé(e), je déteste...*

UNIT 5

Word Page

AUDIO
foucherconnect.fr/23pttpm69

Events *Les événements*

a concert
un concert

a sci-fi festival
un festival de science-fiction

a stage show
un spectacle

a tournament
un tournoi

Places *Les lieux*

a (fun)fair
une fête foraine

a fastfood restaurant
un restaurant rapide

a gym(nasium)
un gymnase

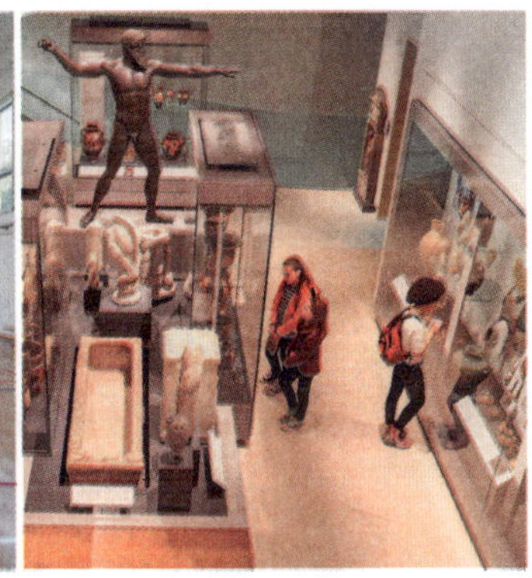

a museum
un musée

a pub
un pub (anglais)

a theme park
un parc d'attractions

a (fancy-dress) party
une fête/soirée (costumée)

a stadium
un stade

Vocabulary

ACTIVITIES *les activités*

go* shopping *faire du shopping*
go* to the cinema *aller au cinéma*
have* a drink *prendre un verre*
have* a party *faire une fête, une soirée*
have* a picnic *faire un pique-nique*
have* lunch *déjeuner*
play badminton *jouer au badminton*
play handball *jouer au handball*
play video games *jouer aux jeux vidéo*
visit *visiter*

Verbs

meet* *se retrouver, se rejoindre*
register *s'inscrire*

Adjectives

busy *occupé(e)*
expensive *cher/chère*
fantastic *fantastique*
free *libre, gratuit*
great *super, génial*

UNIT 5

PROJECT

A2

Invite a friend to do an activity with you

SCENARIO

Vous allez recevoir des élèves anglophones dans votre lycée. Vous souhaitez inviter l'un d'entre eux par téléphone à participer à une activité. Imaginez le dialogue.

A1

Trouver les informations concernant une invitation

- Choisissez ce que vous voudriez faire (activité, lieu, jour, heure) et remplissez la grille suivante.

→ Activity:	→ Place: ....
→ Date:	→ Time: ....

A2

Formuler une invitation

- Formez un binôme (élève A et élève B).
- Entraînez-vous à réaliser le premier dialogue, puis le second.
- Enregistrez vos dialogues.

DIALOGUE 1

Élève A	Élève B
1. Dites bonjour et annoncez-vous.	**1.** Dites bonjour et demandez à votre ami comment il va.
2. Demandez à votre ami(e) s'il/elle voudrait faire l'activité que vous avez choisie.	**2.** Remerciez pour l'invitation. Vous êtes d'accord. Dites ce que vous pensez de cette idée.
3. Proposez de vous retrouver à une heure précise devant le lycée.	**3.** Répondez que ça vous convient et dites au revoir.

DIALOGUE 2

Élève A	Élève B
1. Dites bonjour et annoncez-vous.	**1.** Dites bonjour et demandez à votre ami comment il va.
2. Demandez à votre ami(e) s'il/elle voudrait faire l'activité que vous avez choisie.	**2.** Vous êtes désolé(e) mais vous ne pouvez pas ce jour-là, vous êtes occupé(e).
3. Proposez un autre jour de la semaine.	**3.** Vous êtes d'accord.
4. Proposez de vous retrouver à l'arrêt de bus et dites au revoir.	

CULTURE CLICK 3 AUSTRALIA

a. Arnhem Land

....

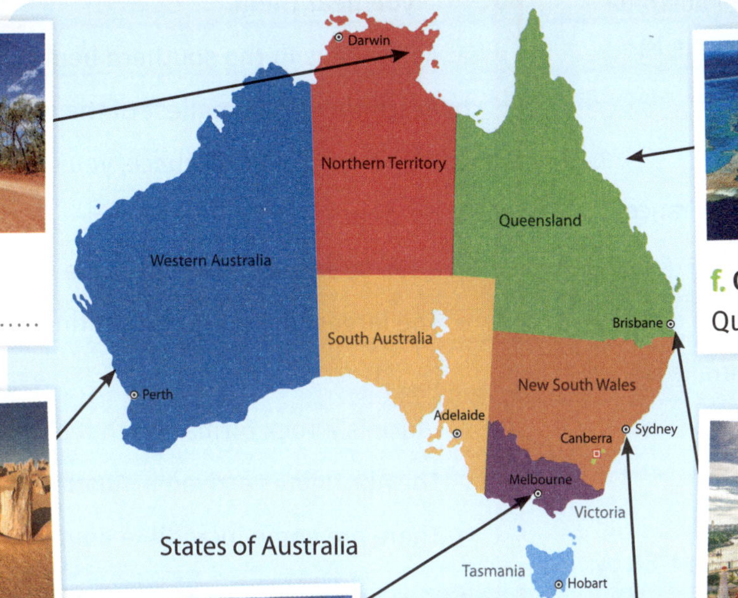

f. Great Barrier Reef
Queensland

b. Pinnacles Desert

....

e. Brisbane

....

c. Melbourne

....

d. Sydney Opera House

....

1 **Look at the map and fill in the names of the Australian states or territories.**

2 41 **Listen and tick the correct answers.**

a. Arnhem land is known for the art and traditions of its First Nations: ☐ inhabitants ☐ visitors

b. In the Pinnacles Desert, you can see hundreds of spectacular limestone pinnacles[1] and you can also spot wild: ☐ kangaroos ☐ emus[2]

c. Melbourne is the: ☐ largest ☐ second largest city in Australia.

d. The Sydney Opera House, located near Harbour Bridge, is one of the world's most famous buildings and a masterpiece of: ☐ 20th ☐ 21st -century architecture.

e. Brisbane has numerous resorts for an exciting: ☐ week ☐ beach holiday.

f. The Great Barrier Reef is the world's largest coral reef and a great place for: ☐ snorkelling ☐ swimming

1 des piliers de calcaire 2 des émeus

3 **Find the English equivalents.**

a. *sauvage:* ....

b. *une station touristique:* ....

c. *un récif de corail:* ....

d. *faire de la plongée avec masque et tuba:* ....

© Éditions Foucher

CULTURE CLICK 3 AUSTRALIA

QUIZ

1. The official name of Australia is the:
- ☐ a. Kingdom of Australia
- ☐ b. United States of Australia
- ☐ c. Commonwealth of Australia

2. The capital city of Australia is:
- ☐ a. Canberra
- ☐ b. Sydney
- ☐ c. Melbourne

3. Australia is ... the size of France:
- ☐ a. 10 times
- ☐ b. 14 times
- ☐ c. 20 times

4. The population of Australia is approximately:
- ☐ a. 14 million
- ☐ b. 24 million
- ☐ c. 34 million

5. Australia was colonized in 1788 by:
- ☐ a. the British
- ☐ b. the Spanish
- ☐ c. the Chinese

6. When it is 10.00 am in Paris, in Sydney it is:
- ☐ a. 4.00 pm
- ☐ b. 8.00 pm
- ☐ c. 10.00 pm

7. The percentage of Australians living on or near the coast is:
- ☐ a. 50%
- ☐ b. 75%
- ☐ c. 90%

8. The Australian flag has:
- ☐ a. 4 stars
- ☐ b. 6 stars
- ☐ c. 8 stars

9. In Australia, you pay in:
- ☐ a. AU dollars
- ☐ b. US dollars
- ☐ c. pounds

10. Who is not Australian?
- ☐ a. Cate Blanchett
- ☐ b. Chris Hemsworth
- ☐ c. Russell Crowe

42 **Listen and check.**

Your score: ..../10

VIDÉO 2:55
Australia | Destination World
foucherconnect.fr/23pttpm26

4 Watch the video and number the sentences in the order you hear them.

a. Australia is in the southern hemisphere. (......)

b. Australia is the smallest of the seven continents. (......)

c. In the Australian Outback, you can see almost 3,000 stars on clear nights. (......)

d. 1,500 species of fish live in the Great Barrier Reef. (......)

e. The largest desert in the continent is the Great Victoria. (......)

f. Uluru is a rock formation that stands 1,100 feet tall. (......)

g. The Aborigines arrived in Australia 50,000 years ago. (......)

h. There are some incredible animals in Australia. (......)

5 Write the names of three animals found only in Australia.

....

....

Aboriginal Art

Aboriginal art has survived for over thousands of years and continues to be one of the oldest art forms practiced today. Aboriginal art consists of symbols. These symbols were used as a means of communication; communication of [Aborigines'] lives on earth, their rituals, food, customs and also to show constellations and for ritual decorations. These works were almost always ceremonial or religious.

https://art-educ4kids.weebly.com.

6 Read the article and answer the questions.

a. How old is Aboriginal art? ....

b. What form does it take? ....

c. What could Aborigines communicate about?

....

....

d. What do you think of this art? ....

7 You can go on the site to learn more about this art and the frequent symbols that were used.

WWW INTERNET
foucherconnect.fr/23pttpm27

© Éditions Foucher

UNIT 6 Team Sports

PROJECT A2+

Create a board game to promote team sports for the International Day of Sport.

A

Name: .... Gobert

Nationality: ....

Sport: ....

Achievement: .... Defensive Player of the Year ▶ .... times

B

Name: .... Rapinoe

Nationality: ....

Sport: ....

Achievement: Women's .... winner ▶ .... times

C

Name: Beauden Barrett

Nationality: ....

Sport: ....

Achievement: World .... of the Year ▶ ....times

1 **Look at the pictures and describe who you see. Try to fill in the missing words.**

2 43 **Listen and check your answers.**

3 **What do you know about these sports? Do you know any other players?**

UNIT 6

Sport is life

ACTIVITY A Break the ice

1 Tick the correct answers.

a. The image represents a: ☐ ice hockey ☐ snowboarding game.
b. There are: ☐ 2 ☐ 3 ☐ 4 teams.
c. In each team, there are: ☐ 3 ☐ 4 ☐ 5 ☐ 6 players.
d. Every player must have a: ☐ racket ☐ stick
e. They play on a: ☐ field ☐ rink
f. The aim is to push the: ☐ puck ☐ ball into the net.

2 Write the letters corresponding to the answers from exercise 1 next to the questions.

1	What is the aim of the game?	......
2	Where do the players play?	......
3	How many players are there in each team?	......
4	What object do they play with?	......
5	How many teams are there in an ice hockey game?	......

WORD BOX
- **an aim** un objectif
- **a field** un terrain
- **a net** un filet
- **a puck** un palet
- **a rink** une patinoire
- **a stick** une crosse, un bâton

ACTIVITY B The prince of England

44 Listen and answer the questions.

a. What's his name? ....
b. What sport does he play? ....
c. What nationality is he? ....
d. What team does he play for? ....
e. What can he do? ....
f. What's his nickname? ....
g. Why does he have this nickname? ....

GRAMMAR SPOT

a. I must wear my helmet.
b. The defence can stop the offence.
c. I mustn't take my helmet off.

Quelle phrase exprime :
– une interdiction ? ......
– une obligation ? ......
– une possibilité ? ......

Training ex. 4 & 6 p. 62

ACTION 1

Poser des questions sur un athlète ou un sport et y répondre A2+

Work in pairs. Student A: Ask questions to find the name of an athlete. Student B: Go to p. 116 and use the information on the card to answer your partner's questions.
Then switch roles. Student B: Ask questions to find the name of a sport. Student A: Go to p. 119.

© Éditions Foucher

Give your best shot

ACTIVITY C Stay safe

1 Look at the picture and fill in the missing labels.

jersey • helmet • knee pads • shoulder pads • cleats

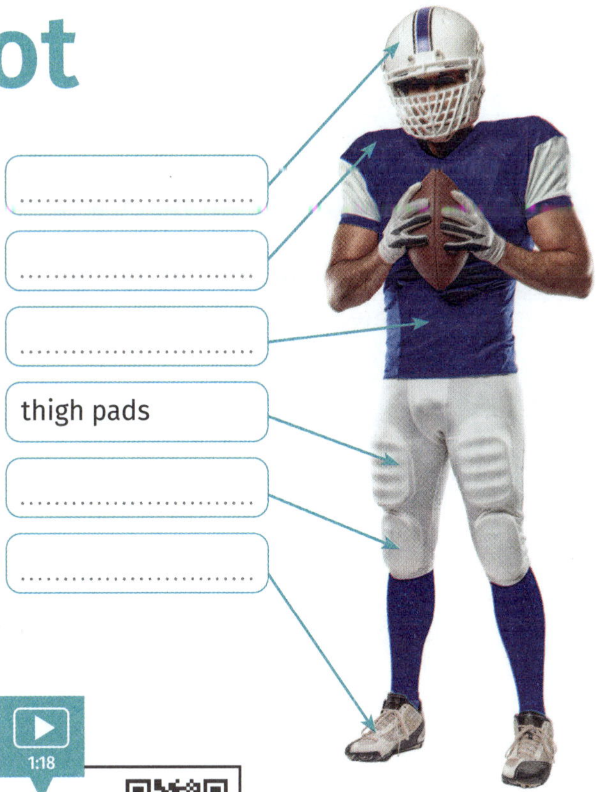

2 45 Listen and tick True or False. Correct orally when it's false.

a. Thomas plays soccer. ☐ True ☐ False
b. Thomas must wear pads to protect himself. ☐ True ☐ False
c. Thomas can't wear a helmet. ☐ True ☐ False

ACTIVITY D Touchdown!

1:18
VIDÉO
A Beginner's Guide to American Football
foucherconnect.fr/23pttpm24

1 Complete the sentences. Watch the video and check.

players • points • opponent • teams • passing • rushing • score

a. American football is a game played by two .... of 11 ....
b. The aim is to move the ball into the ....'s end zone to .... a touchdown.
c. They play by .... the ball through the air or by .... the ball along the ground.
d. The team with the most .... wins the game.

WORD BOX
- **need** avoir besoin de
- **an opponent** un adversaire
- **pass** passer
- **rush** (se) précipiter
- **score** marquer

2 Watch again and circle the correct answers.

a. Players (*must* / *can*) pass the ball through the air.
b. Players (*must* / *mustn't*) pass the ball using their feet.
c. The offence (*must* / *can*) move the ball at least 10 yards[1] down.
d. The defence (*can* / *can't*) stop the offence.
e. Players (*can* / *can't*) kick the ball between the posts.

1 a yard = 0,9 meters

ACTION 2

Écrire des phrases simples sur les règles d'un sport A2

Use the information to write five sentences about hurling rules. Use *must*, *mustn't* or *can*.

Obligation	Prohibition (⊘)	Possibility
- Use your hands and feet - Be fast	- Hit the opponent	- Catch the ball in the air - Block the opponent's shots with a stick

Team spirit

ACTIVITY E The eye of the tiger

1 **Look at the picture and say what you know about this athlete.**

2 46 **Listen and circle the correct answers.**

Michael Jordan was a (*leader / follower*) who inspired his teammates and pushed them to be (*slower / better*). Jordan's competitiveness made a (*difference / reference*) because he wanted to play and (*win / lose*) as a team. One of his mottoes was: Never (*give up / get up*).

How To Be Like Mike: [2] lessons from Michael Jordan

You Can't Do It Alone

"Talent wins games, but teamwork and intelligence win championships." – Michael Jordan

Throughout the '80s, Jordan racked up a ton of personal achievements (scoring titles, league MVP awards, and "Defensive Player of the Year"). But no championships. Those didn't come until he had the help of Scottie Pippen, Horace Grant, and Phil Jackson.

Demand The Best From Your Team

Fred Lynch, one of Jordan's high school coaches, recalls that Jordan was demanding even as a teenager: "He'd get on his teammates all the time. He hasn't changed that. What he always expected was everybody played the game as hard as he played it. "Expecting the best in others helps bring it out in them.

https://tsbasketball.com.

3 **Read the text and find the English equivalents.**

a. *seul*: ....

b. *tout le long de*: ....

c. *accumulé*: ....

d. *des réussites*: ....

e. *(s')attendre* (à): ....

f. *faire ressortir*: ....

4 **Tick True or False. When it's false, circle the correct sentences in the text.**

a. You can win without your teammates. ☐ True ☐ False

b. During the '80s, Jordan won many championships. ☐ True ☐ False

c. He won championships thanks to his teammates. ☐ True ☐ False

d. For Jordan, players must work as hard as he does. ☐ True ☐ False

e. Jordan demanded the best from his teammates to make them succeed. ☐ True ☐ False

WORD BOX

- **demanding** exigeant
- **give* up** abandonner
- **make* a difference** faire la différence
- **a motto** une devise
- **push to** pousser à

LET'S GO FURTHER!!!

47 **Listen to the audio. Present the sport and explain the importance of teamwork in it.**

ACTION 3

MÉDIATION A2+

Rendre compte d'un ensemble de documents

Recap in French what you have understood from the audio and the text about Michael Jordan.

AUDIO foucherconnect.fr/23pttpm43

in TUNE

A 48 **Écoutez et répétez les mots suivants.**

must **/mʌst/** mustn't **/mʌsnt/**

B 49 **Écoutez et cochez les modaux utilisés.**

	a	b	c	d	e
/mʌst/ must	☐	☐	☐	☐	☐
/mʌsnt/ mustn't	☐	☐	☐	☐	☐

Challenge!

1 **Listez le plus vite possible tous les sports d'équipe de ce dessin.**

2 **Écrivez les verbes correspondants sous les images.**

score • pass • catch • block • rush

a. ....

b. ....

c. ....

d. ....

e. ....

3 **Reliez chaque mot à sa définition.**

a. a ball •	• **1.** an object to protect the head
b. a helmet •	• **2.** a sports playing area
c. a field •	• **3.** a round object you play with
d. cleats •	• **4.** a shirt with a number used in sports
e. a jersey •	• **5.** special shoes to play on a soccer field

© Éditions Foucher

4 **Entourez la bonne réponse.**

a. You (*must / mustn't*) wear flip-flops* to play football.
b. Basketball players (*must / mustn't*) wear a helmet.
c. Rugby players (*can / must*) kick the ball.
d. Football players (*can / mustn't*) use their hands.
e. Ice hockey players (*must / mustn't*) use a stick.
f. A basketball player (*can / can't*) block an opponent.

* *tongs*

5 50 **Écoutez et complétez les mots manquants.**

Rugby rules

The aim of the game is to .... more points than the .... in 80 minutes.

The .... with the greater number of points at full time is announced as the winner.

The team with the ball .... move the ball up the field in 'phases of play'. The ball .... never be passed forward but players .... run forwards with the ball or .... the ball forward.

6 **Écrivez cinq règles du jeu de votre sport préféré.**

a. ....
b. ....
c. ....
d. ....
e. ....

7 **Reliez chaque question à sa réponse.**

a. What's her name? •	• 1. She is American.
b. What sport does she play? •	• 2. Her name is Candace Parker.
c. What's her nationality? •	• 3. She plays basketball.
d. What team does she play for? •	• 4. She plays for Chicago.
e. What can she do? •	• 5. She can shoot three-point shots.

TIPS LANGUAGE

Exprimer l'obligation : *must* + BV

Players must work hard.
Les joueurs doivent travailler dur.

Exprimer l'interdiction : *mustn't* + BV

You mustn't hit your opponent.
Tu ne dois pas frapper ton adversaire.

Exprimer une possibilité : *can* + BV

Players can kick the ball.
Les joueurs peuvent frapper le ballon.

© Éditions Foucher

UNIT 6

Word Page

AUDIO
foucherconnect.fr/23pttpm44

Equipment *Équipement*

a ball
un ballon

cleats
des chaussures à crampons

a field
un terrain

a helmet
un casque

a jersey
un maillot

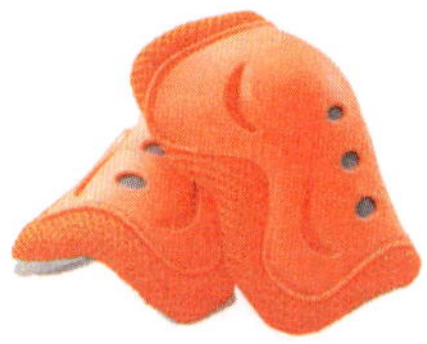
a knee pad
une genouillère

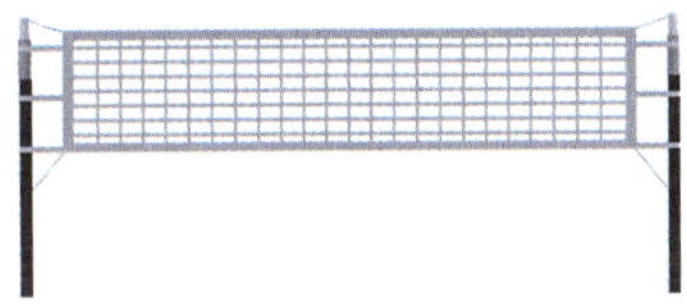
a net
un filet

a puck
un palet

a racket
une raquette

a rink
une patinoire

a shoulder pad
une épaulière

a stick
une crosse

Actions *Actions*

block
contrer

catch*
attraper

hit*
frapper

kick
frapper avec le pied

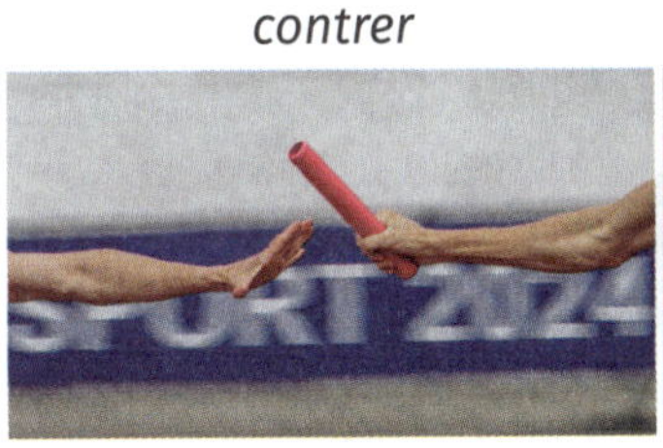

pass
passer

rush
se déplacer vite

score
marquer

win*
gagner

Vocabulary

Nouns

an aim *un objectif*
a championship *un championnat*
a defence *une défense*
an offence *une attaque*
an opponent *un adversaire*
a player *un joueur*
a team *une équipe*
a teammate *un co-équipier*

Verbs

give* up *abandonner*
lose* *perdre*
protect *protéger*
push *pousser*
use *utiliser*
wear* *porter*

UNIT 6

A2+

Create a board game

PROJECT

SCENARIO

À l'occasion de la Journée internationale du sport, votre classe crée un jeu pour promouvoir les sports d'équipe. À l'aide du modèle, créez votre propre jeu de plateau.

A2+

Faire des recherches sur des sports d'équipe

- Une fois la classe divisée en deux, trouvez des informations sur plusieurs sports d'équipe (athlètes les plus connu(e)s, règles d'un sport, équipements…).

A2+

Rédiger des questions

- Rédigez chaque question et sa réponse sur une carte, selon les modèles ci-dessous (30 questions minimum).

foucherconnect.fr/23pttpm46

A2+

Jouer au jeu de plateau

- Formez un paquet avec vos cartes, puis échangez votre paquet de cartes avec celui de l'autre équipe pour jouer.
- Jouez au jeu créé par l'autre groupe, en deux équipes (équipe A et équipe B), à l'aide du plateau de jeu proposé.

DOCUMENT
foucherconnect.fr/23pttpm45

Règles du jeu

Un élève de l'équipe A lance le dé*, avance d'autant de cases que le nombre indiqué et répond à la question qu'un élève de l'équipe B aura posée.

Si la réponse est bonne, l'équipe rejoue. Si elle n'est pas bonne, c'est au tour de l'autre équipe. La carte sera replacée sous le paquet.

La première équipe qui arrive sur la case « Finish » et qui aura répondu correctement à la question posée a gagné la partie.

Proposez à vos camarades de l'établissement de jouer au jeu et de tester leurs connaissances.

*si vous n'avez pas de dé, vous pouvez en utiliser un en ligne :

INTERNET
foucherconnect.fr/23pttpm25

MÉTHODE 3

S'exprimer à l'oral

1 Identifiez le sujet sur lequel vous allez vous exprimer.
- Pensez aux mots que vous connaissez sur le sujet.
- Utilisez-les pour développer quelques idées.

2 Écoutez bien votre interlocuteur et réagissez.
- Repérez les questions, les mots clés.
- N'hésitez pas à lui demander de répéter si vous n'êtes pas sûr(e) d'avoir compris. **(A)**
- Répondez à ses questions et donnez votre avis. **(B)**

3 N'ayez pas peur de parler.
- Il est normal de faire des erreurs quand on apprend.
- Parlez calmement, ne vous précipitez pas.
- Faites des phrases courtes.

4 Soignez votre prononciation.
Pensez à bien prononcer (accent et intonation). Vous pouvez vous entraîner sur des sites en ligne comme www.fromtexttospeech.com, www.naturalreaders.com…

5 Exprimez-vous naturellement.
- Apprenez quelques expressions pour exprimer vos émotions, réactions… **(C)**
- Utilisez des « gapfillers » pour vous donner le temps de la réflexion et rendre votre parole plus naturelle. **(D)**

6 Lancez-vous !

À retenir

A Faire répéter	B Donner son avis	C Exprimer ses réactions	D Utiliser des *gap-fillers*
- Sorry, I didn't understand. *Désolé(e), je n'ai pas compris.* - Can you repeat that, please? *Pouvez-vous répéter, s'il vous plaît ?* - Can you speak slowly, please? *Pouvez-vous parler lentement, s'il vous plaît ?* - Speak up, please. *Parlez plus fort, s'il vous plaît.*	- I think… *Je pense…* - I believe… *Je crois…* - For me… *Pour moi…* - In my opinion… *À mon avis…* - For example *par exemple* - I agree / disagree *je suis d'accord / je ne suis pas d'accord* - Me too / Me neither *Moi aussi / Moi non plus*	- Great! *Super !* - Fantastic! *Génial !* - Incredible! *Incroyable !* - Terrible! *Horrible !* - I'm pleased / happy. *Je suis content(e)/ heureux(se).* - It's good. *C'est bien/ bon.*	- Er…. *Heu….* - Well… *Bon/Eh bien…* - You know. *Vous savez/ comprenez.* - You see. *Vous voyez.* - Let me think. *Laissez-moi réfléchir.* - So… *Donc/Alors…*

AUDIO
foucherconnect.fr/23pttpm47

Entraînez-vous !

1 **Reliez les énoncés aux types de phrases.**

a. Sorry, I didn't understand. •	• **1.** Gap-fillers
b. I think he is a great musician. •	• **2.** Asking to repeat
c. How fantastic! •	• **3.** Asking questions
d. Er… I don't know…You see … •	• **4.** Expressing reactions
e. What series do you like? •	• **5.** Expressing points of view

2 **Écoutez la conversation et complétez. Puis entourez les *gap-fillers*.**

foucherconnect.fr/23pttpm48

a. Robin: It's my birthday next week.

b. Samia: ....

c. Robin: I'll have… er… an evening party at my home or… er… a picnic in a park. I don't know exactly.
....

d. Samia: Well… You know… I like picnics but I would .... an evening party at your house.

e. Robin: Yes, ...Why not a theme party?

f. Samia: Yes, that's .... What about organizing a zombie party?

g. Robin: Can you .... please?

h. Samia: I think it could be fun to organize a zombie party.

i. Robin: Yes! Fantastic! Let me think… We could decorate my room!

j. Samia: Yes, ..., we could decorate your room with zombie ....
and prepare strange zombie .... I can help you!

k. Robin: Thank you! I'll be .... to prepare the party with you! It's going to be fun!

3 **Relisez le dialogue complété et indiquez dans quelle réplique (a-j):**

a. le locuteur donne ses préférences : ....

b. le locuteur est d'accord avec son interlocuteur : ....

c. le locuteur n'a pas compris : ....

d. le locuteur donne des exemples : ....

e. le locuteur exprime son contentement : ....

4 **Discutez avec votre voisin d'un des sujets ci-dessous. Essayez de parler chacun à votre tour en enchaînant un maximum de répliques.**

Sujet 1 : The next Olympic Games.
(When? Where? What to see? Your favourite individual sports / team sports? Your favourite champions? Do you practice sports?)

Sujet 2 : Living and working in the USA.
(Where would you like to live? What job would you like to do? What could you see / visit?)

© Éditions Foucher

UNIT 7

Present Your Internship

PROJECT B1

As part of an eTwinning project, you exchange with pen pals about your internship in order to promote work experience.

A

Hello! I am Louis. During my internship last year, I was an .... in a clothes shop. Clara was my ....

B

Hi, I am Katie. Two months ago, I worked in a restaurant. I loved that ....! I did various .... and I discovered a passion for cooking.

C

Hey, I am Yanis. I did my last internship in an air conditioning .... and they hired* me! The job is great!

*embaucher

1 (51) **Listen and fill in the bubbles with:**

tutor • internship • company • intern • tasks

2 Tick the elements corresponding to the jobs.

a. A shop assistant → ☐ a shop ☐ a restaurant ☐ a cash register[1] ☐ a factory[2]

b. A chef → ☐ a restaurant ☐ meat and vegetables ☐ a garage ☐ knives[3]

c. An air conditioning engineer → ☐ outside ☐ inside ☐ knives ☐ tools[4]

1 une caisse enregistreuse 2 une usine 3 des couteaux 4 des outils

3 Say where you did your last internship.

© Éditions Foucher

UNIT 7

Where did you work?

ACTIVITY A Company ID

1 Look at the picture and describe it.

2 52 Listen to Florence, a mechanic, and fill in the information.

Workplace	....
Location	....
Number of employees	....
Working days	....
Working hours	....

3 53 Listen and underline the correct answers.

a. The company was 10 minutes' (*walk* / *drive*) from my house.
b. There were 15 employees, including (*2* / *4* / *12*) interns.
c. My tutor was the (*boss* / *supervisor* / *manager*).
d. My internship lasted (*3* / *6* / *8*) weeks.

WORD BOX

- **check** vérifier
- **greet** accueillir

GRAMMAR SPOT

a. I worked in a garage last June.
b. There were 15 employees.

À quel temps sont les verbes soulignés ?
☐ *au présent* ☐ *au prétérit*

La terminaison d'un verbe régulier (phrase a) est : ....

Le verbe de la phrase b est un verbe :
☐ *régulier* ☐ *irrégulier*

Entourez le repère de temps.

Le prétérit exprime une action :
☐ *en train de se dérouler*
☐ *passée, datée, terminée*

Training ex. 3 & 5 p. 71

ACTIVITY B Let's get to work!

1 54 Listen to Matt's tutor and fill in the blanks with the following verbs.

greeted • swept • tidied • assisted

a. He .... customers.
b. He .... the shelves*.
c. He .... the floor.
d. He .... me in taking customers' payments.

**étagères*

2 What about you? What tasks did you do during your internship? Write at least three sentences.

....
....
....
....
....
....

ACTION 1

A2 **Présenter une entreprise et les tâches effectuées par le stagiaire**

Go on p. 120. Orally present one of the companies and the tasks done by the intern.

© Éditions Foucher

Work experiences

ACTIVITY C Talking about an internship

1 55 **Match Paul's questions with Daisy's answers. Then, listen and check.**

a. How long did your internship last? •
b. What was your schedule? •
c. Did you eat in the shopping centre restaurants? •
d. What type of tasks did you do? •

• 1. It lasted 6 weeks.
• 2. The first week, I answered the telephone and sent invoices. The following weeks, I filed documents.
• 3. I started at 10 AM and finished at 7 PM.
• 4. No, I didn't. I had lunch in the staffroom.

2 56 **Listen and underline what Daisy says about her internship.**

various activities – interesting tasks – uninteresting tasks – great, relaxed atmosphere – tense and uncomfortable atmosphere – rude and unfriendly employees – nice, helpful employees

GRAMMAR SPOT

a. I didn't cook.

La phrase **a** *est à la forme:*
☐ *affirmative* ☐ *négative*

L'ordre des mots est:
sujet + ... + BV.

b. How long did your internship last?

À la forme interrogative, on utilise: (Mot interrogatif) + ... + *sujet* + ... + ?

Training ex. 6 & 7 p. 72

ACTIVITY D A bad experience

1 57 **Listen and complete Zach's answers.**

My internship was not a .... experience. I worked in a restaurant kitchen. The schedule was very .... because I started early and finished late. The days were very .... and I felt really .... The atmosphere was .... because the staff .... get along*. I felt ....

The tasks were .... as well. I didn't cook but mainly cleaned and did the washing up. I will not do another internship in that restaurant. I didn't learn anything and felt really ....

* *bien s'entendre*

WORD BOX

- **a schedule** un emploi du temps
- **staff** le personnel/les membres du personnel

2 **Say if the sentences are right or wrong and justify your answers.**

a. The schedule was cool.

....

b. The staff were not friends.

....

c. Zach felt great about his internship.

....

ACTION 2

A2 **Comprendre une présentation de stage et en écrire un compte rendu**

AUDIO foucherconnect.fr/23pttpm15

Listen to Helen and Kate's experiences and write what you have understood.

UNIT 7

Feedback

ACTIVITY E Students' impressions

Here's what students said about their internship experience...

"I learned that customer service is hard. You cannot please everyone. There are people in this world that are simply difficult. I also learned to work in a team. I learned not to be afraid to ask a lot of questions too. By asking questions I got answers."

"At the start of the internship I was often frustrated. It was difficult having to learn so much about the company, while still trying to be competent and make a good impression."

"First of all, although[1] it is normal to be on time for work, it is not that easy to show up on time for six or eight weeks. I got tired and I had to manage my sleep and the use of my mobile in the evening. Towards[2] the end, I went to bed very early and almost did not check my phone before sleeping. But I did it; I finished my internship without being late once! And I'm very proud of myself for that!

1 *bien que* 2 *vers*

1 Read the document and tick the correct answers.

a. The subject is: ☐ internship ☐ school experiences.

b. The testimonies* are: ☐ tutors' ☐ interns' comments.

* *témoignages*

2 Find the English equivalents.

a. *le service client* (Ann) ....

b. *ne pas avoir peur* (Ann) ....

c. *faire bonne impression* (Olivia) ....

d. *arriver* (Leo) ....

e. *fier(e)* (Leo) ....

3 Answer the questions with full sentences.

a. What were the three things Ann learned?

....

b. What was Olivia's feeling and why?

....

c. What did Leo realise during his internship?

....

LET'S GO FURTHER!!!

Watch the video and write a summary in French of what you understood.

0:44
VIDÉO
Year 10
Work Experience
foucherconnect.fr/23pttpm16

ACTION 3

MÉDIATION A2+

Rendre compte de témoignages de stage

Écrivez un compte rendu en français de ce que vous avez compris du document (nature, thème principal et idées les plus importantes).

AUDIO
foucherconnect.fr/23pttpm02

in TUNE

A 58 **Écoutez et répétez les verbes suivants.**

/t/ worked **/d/** answered **/id/** lasted

B 59 **Placez les mots dans la bonne colonne. Écoutez et vérifiez.**

asked – loved – helped – greeted – started – stayed – assisted – finished – called – hired

/t/	/d/	/id/
....	....	....
....	....	....
....	....	....
....	....	....

1 **Complétez chaque mot avec les voyelles manquantes et traduisez-les.**

_nt_rnsh_p → .... _nt_rn → .... c_mp_n_ → .... t_sks → ....

2 **Placez le vocabulaire sous les images.**

greet customers • prepare tools • answer the telephone • cook

....

....

....

....

3 **Complétez avec les verbes de l'exercice 2 conjugués au prétérit.**

a. Anne was a shop assistant; ....

b. Tom worked in a restaurant; he .... dishes.

c. Before doing a task, first you .... the ....

d. As an intern in an office, I .... a lot.

4 **Challenge!**

Vous avez deux minutes pour trouver autant de mots que possible en relation avec votre dernier stage.

5 **Reliez les marqueurs de temps à leur traduction.**

a. yesterday • • **1.** *l'an dernier*
b. last year • • **2.** *pendant mon dernier stage*
c. during my last internship • • **3.** *hier*
d. two months ago • • **4.** *il y a 2 mois*

© Éditions Foucher

6 **Conjuguez les verbes au prétérit simple à la forme affirmative (+), négative (-) ou interrogative (?).**

a. Paul .... in Sainsbury's. (work +)

b. Their internship .... four weeks. (last +)

c. Katy and Mary .... in the same company. (work -)

d. My supervisor .... very happy with me. (be +)

e. When .... you .... your internship. (start ?)

7 **Racontez la journée de Tom lors de son dernier stage.**

TIPS LANGUAGE

Le prétérit simple

Exprime une action ou un état daté, passé, terminé.
On l'utilise souvent avec des marqueurs de temps comme *two years ago, last month, yesterday, two hours ago...*

Forme affirmative

- **Verbes réguliers : BV + -ed**

My internship **lasted** 6 weeks. *Mon stage a duré 6 semaines.*

- **Verbes irréguliers :** *cf. liste en rabat de couverture*

I got bored during my internship. *Je me suis ennuyé pendant mon stage.*

Forme interrogative

(pronom interrogatif) + did + sujet + BV + (complément) +?

How long **did** your internship last? *Combien de temps a duré ton stage ?*

Forme négative

didn't + BV

My internship **didn't** last long. *Mon stage n'a pas duré longtemps.*

UNIT 7

Word Page

AUDIO
foucherconnect.fr/23pttpm03

Work places *Les lieux de travail*

an office
un bureau

a shop
un magasin

a workshop
un atelier

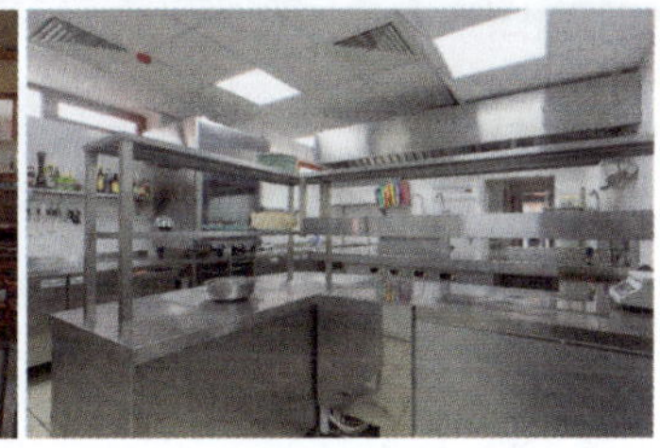

a kitchen
une cuisine

Professional tasks *Les tâches professionnelles*

answer the telephone
répondre au téléphone

cook
cuisiner

dispatch orders
expédier des commandes

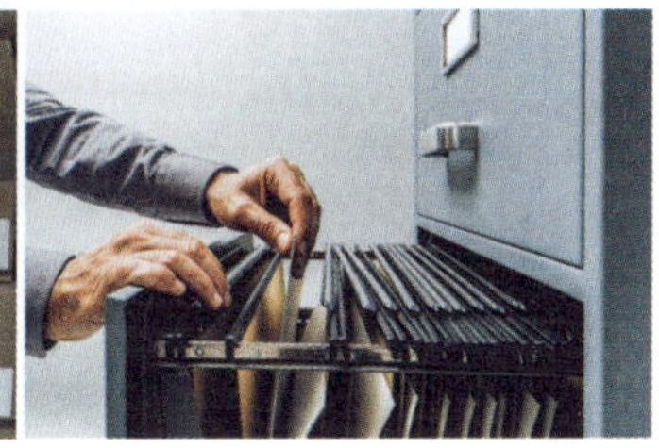

file
classer

fix
réparer

manufacture products
fabriquer des produits

sweep*
balayer

tidy
ranger

Tools *Les outils*

a cash register
une caisse enregistreuse

a computer
un ordinateur

a printer
une imprimante

a screwdriver
un tournevis

Vocabulary

Nouns

an internship *un stage*
an invoice *une facture*
staff *le personnel*
a tutor *un tuteur*
a workplace *un lieu de travail*

Verbs

get* on well *bien s'entendre*
leave* *partir, quitter un lieu*
start *commencer*
take* somebody's payment *encaisser le paiement de quelqu'un*

UNIT 7

PROJECT

A2+

Present your internship

SCENARIO

Dans le cadre d'un projet eTwinning, vous présentez à vos correspondants une de vos expériences en tant que stagiaire en entreprise.

A2

Compléter la fiche profil du stage

- Choisissez un de vos stages puis complétez les informations correspondantes.

→ Name and type of the company: ....

....

→ Location: ....

→ Number of employees: ....

→ Name of the tutor and position in the company: ....

....

→ Duration of the internship: ....

→ Your working hours: ....

A2+

Présenter les tâches professionnelles

- En vous aidant éventuellement d'un dictionnaire, indiquez au moins 3 activités que vous avez réalisées.

→ Tasks

1 ....

2 ....

3 ....

A2+

Donner son opinion sur un stage

- Préparez au moins 2 phrases en donnant vos impressions sur votre stage.

....

....

B1

Présenter un stage

- À l'aide de vos notes, présentez oralement votre stage à vos correspondants eTwinning.

CULTURE CLICK 4 FAMOUS AMERICAN LANDMARKS

a. The Space Needle

....

b. The Golden Gate Bridge

....

c. *Cloud Gate*

....

d. The Alamo

....

e. The Lincoln Memorial

....

f. The Liberty Bell

....

1 (60) **Listen and write the names of the cities under the famous places.**

San Francisco • Washington • Seattle • Chicago • Philadelphia • San Antonio

2 (60) **Listen again and tick the correct answers.**

a. The Space Needle is a: ☐ 505 ☐ 605 -foot-tall tower with a view of the city skyline.
b. The Golden Gate Bridge opened in: ☐ 1937 ☐ 1957
c. *Cloud Gate* is a: ☐ painting ☐ sculpture by British artist Anish Kapoor.
d. The Alamo in San Antonio is the place where American hero Davy Crockett died in: ☐ 1826 ☐ 1836.
e. The Lincoln Memorial was built to honour: ☐ the 16th ☐ the 26th US president, Abraham Lincoln.
f. The Liberty Bell is an iconic symbol of: ☐ American ☐ British independence.

QUIZ

1. **The capital city of the USA is:**
   - ☐ a. Washington, DC
   - ☐ b. Chicago
   - ☐ c. New York
2. **The Empire State Building was finished in:**
   - ☐ a. 1931
   - ☐ b. 1936
   - ☐ c. 1941
3. **The longest bridge in the USA is in the state of:**
   - ☐ a. California
   - ☐ b. Louisiana
   - ☐ c. Nevada
4. **Las Vegas's nickname is:**
   - ☐ a. The Magic City
   - ☐ b. The city that never sleeps
   - ☐ c. Sin City
5. **In the USA, the Hot Springs National Park is in:**
   - ☐ a. Arkansas
   - ☐ b. Florida
   - ☐ c. Connecticut
6. **Mount Rushmore is:**
   - ☐ a. a castle
   - ☐ b. a sculpture
   - ☐ c. a skyscraper
7. **Route 66 originally ran from Chicago to:**
   - ☐ a. Las Vegas
   - ☐ b. Los Angeles
   - ☐ c. San Francisco
8. **In the USA, One World Trade Center opened in:**
   - ☐ a. 2006
   - ☐ b. 2013
   - ☐ c. 2014
9. **Monument Valley has served as a setting for many:**
   - ☐ a. comedies
   - ☐ b. sci-fi films
   - ☐ c. westerns
10. **Diamond Head in Hawaii is:**
    - ☐ a. a volcano
    - ☐ b. a mountain
    - ☐ c. a beach

61 **Listen and check.**

Your score: ..../10

Yosemite National Park

The jewel in the crown of California's national parks, Yosemite has been stunning visitors since the first two travellers laid eyes on it in 1855. Now, every year over four million people stand in awe of its unique natural treasures [...] Carved into the center of the Sierra Nevada Mountains by ancient geological forces, Yosemite's splendor and biodiversity are so grand that it was even designated a UNESCO World Heritage site in 1984.

www.visittheusa.co.uk.

3 Read the text and answer the questions.

a. When did the first travellers discover Yosemite National Park? ....

b. How many people visit the park every year? ....

c. Where is Yosemite National Park? ....

....

d. What happened in 1984? ....

....

1:37

VIDÉO
5 Facts about the Statue of Liberty

foucherconnect.fr/23pttpm29

4 Watch the video and tick the correct answers.

a. The Statue of Liberty's real name is:
☐ Miss America ☐ Liberty Enlightening the World

b. The spikes represent: ☐ the seven seas and continents
☐ the first seven colonies

c. The statue is modelled after the architect's:
☐ sister ☐ mother

d. Every year, she gets struck by lightning:
☐ 500 ☐ 600 times.

e. Her original colour was: ☐ copper ☐ green

UNIT 8 Be Green!

PROJECT A2+

For World Environment Day, create a poster to encourage people to protect the environment

* un bronzage

1 **Look at the picture and describe what you see.**

2 **Tick the right answers.**

a. The document is: ☐ a photograph ☐ a cartoon
b. It is set in the: ☐ Arctic Ocean ☐ Pacific Ocean
c. The two polar bears on the left: ☐ look* surprised ☐ don't look surprised
d. The bear on the right is: ☐ a panda ☐ a polar bear
e. It says it is black and white because: ☐ it is a panda ☐ it is tanned
f. It is because of: ☐ climate change ☐ Covid-19

* *avoir l'air*

UNIT 8

How to go green?

ACTIVITY A Tips for a better environment

1 **Write the actions under the right pictures.**

collect rain water • go electric • plant a tree • use natural energy • sort your rubbish

a.	b.	c.	d.	e. ....

2 62 **Listen and complete.**

a. You should sort your waste in order to ....
or reuse it and .... carbon emissions.

b. You should plant a tree. Trees give off ....
and can absorb carbon dioxide.

c. You should use electric means of ....
They have a big effect on .... quality.

d. You should use natural energy like wind or solar
.... because .... is a big source
of carbon emissions.

e. You should collect rain to save ....

GRAMMA SPOT

a. **You should plant a tree.**
b. **You shouldn't buy plastic products.**

Soulignez le modal qui exprime le conseil dans les phrases a et b.

Où se place le modal ? ☐ *avant le verbe* ☐ *après le verbe*

Training ex. 6 p.

WORD BOX

- **give* off** émettre
- **a means of transport** un moyen de transport
- **rubbish/waste** des déchets
- **save** économiser
- **sort** trier
- **turn on/turn off** allumer/éteindre
- **wind power** l'énergie éolienne (vent)

ACTIVITY B How to help the ecosystem

63 **Tick true or false. Then listen and check your score.**

a. You should turn off the TV when you're not watching it. ☐ True ☐ False
b. You should travel by plane. ☐ True ☐ False
c. You shouldn't buy plastic products. ☐ True ☐ False
d. Trees clean the air. ☐ True ☐ False
e. You shouldn't turn off the water while you're brushing your teeth. ☐ True ☐ False
f. You shouldn't eat too much meat. ☐ True ☐ False
g. Pollution is good for the environment. ☐ True ☐ False
h. You should use lamps instead of sunlight. ☐ True ☐ False

Your score: ..... / 8

LET'S GO FURTHER!!!

Answer this quiz to check how "green" you are.

QUIZ

foucherconnect.fr/23pttpm19

ACTION 1

Rédiger un quiz sur le thème de l'environnement A2

Write a True or False quiz like in Activity B. Use "should" and "shouldn't". Then ask a classmate to do it and check her/his answers.

Example: You should take the stairs instead of the lift. ☐ True ☐ False

Take action

ACTIVITY C Save water

VIDÉO 2:08
Top 10 water saving tips
foucherconnect.fr/23pttpm20

1 Watch the video and complete the tips.

a. .... the tap .... when you brush your teeth	b. Have .... instead of	c. Use the “eco” setting on your	d. .... a leaking tap	e. .... plants with a watering can

2 Watch again and match each recommendation with its benefits.

- a. Turn the tap off •
- b. Don’t take a bath •
- c. Use the “eco” setting • on your dishwasher
- d. Fix a leaking tap •

- • 1. It saves 504 bottles per week
- • 2. It fills up 5.5 fire engines
- • 3. It saves 25% of your energy bill
- • 4. It saves 23 litres

GRAMMAR SPOT

a. **Wake up.**

b. **Don’t burn our future.**

Entourez la forme affirmative et soulignez la forme négative de l’impératif.

Ces phrases expriment :
☐ *une possibilité* ☐ *un ordre / une consigne* ☐ *une recommandation*

Training ex. 7 p. 82

ACTIVITY D Protest

64 **Listen and circle the words you hear.**

More and more young people are (*protesting* / *contesting*) against climate change around the world. With the slogans on their (*placards* / *blackboards*), they (*demand* / *plan*) urgent action to save the planet. 15-year-old Greta Thunberg started the movement in 2018 in Stockholm. It quickly went (*mobile* / *global*).

ACTION 2

A2 **Répondre à un tweet sur la journée mondiale de l’environnement**

Write five tips to answer Gabriel’s tweet. Use the imperative form.

Gabriel @GreenGabriel

Today is World Environment Day! Give 5 tips to save electricity!

10:55 AM . Jun 5, 2023

29k Retweets **1,954** Quote Tweets **330k** Likes

Name @Username • Jun 5 ...

Your tweet here! ....

....

....

Green teens

ACTIVITY E Green high school

1 **Read the text and underline where, who and what it is about.**

2 **Find the English equivalents:**

a. *des adolescents* (titre): ....

b. *faire prendre conscience* (§2): ....

c. *des problèmes* (§2): ....

d. *mis en œuvre* (§3): ....

e. *des substances polluantes* (§3): ....

f. *le personnel de restauration* (§4): ....

g. *des ordures* (§4): ....

3 **Explain in French what you have understood from the text.**

French Teens Foster[1] a Greener High School in Toulouse

In Toulouse, in the southwest of France, a group of 30 students is working towards the ecological transition of their high school. [...]

The small group of students started brainstorming ideas with two main goals: limiting the school's impact on the environment and raising awareness about climate issues. [...]

So far, around 40 [actions] have been implemented over the last two years: creating a biodiversity corridor, designing an exhibition to present pollutants and their green alternatives, inviting climate scientists to speak at conferences at the school, installing parking for bikes.

In the canteen, the students and the catering staff have worked together to inform the public about the amount of trash generated every month through communication campaigns, and as a result, waste has been reduced by 50% over two years.

1 foster: *promouvoir*

Pauline Bandelier, RFI, 31/03/2021.

ACTIVITY F Bye bye plastic bags

1 **Watch the video (up to 1'43") and find the information.**

Names:	....
Ages:	....
Place:	....

1:43
VIDÉO
Bali sisters say 'Bye Bye Plastic Bags'
foucherconnect.fr/23pttpm21

2 **Answer the questions.**

a. What's the name of their foundation? ....

b. How old were they when they started the foundation? ....

c. Why did they start the foundation? ....

d. What result did they get? ....

ACTION 3

MÉDIATION A2

Rendre compte d'un court reportage

Watch the video (up to 1'19") and explain in French the common points and the differences with the video from Activity F.

1:19
VIDÉO
Teens around the world demand action on climate change
foucherconnect.fr/23pttpm22

TRAINING

AUDIO foucherconnect.fr/23pttpm40

in TUNE

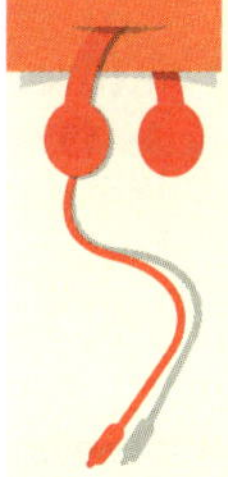

A 65 **Écoutez et répétez les mots suivants.**

/ʃ/: shower   /tʃ/: change

B 66 **Écoutez et cochez la bonne prononciation des lettres soulignées.**

a. should b. pollution c. natural d. rubbish e. beach f. temperature g. ocean

	a	b	c	d	e	f	g
/ʃ/	☐	☐	☐	☐	☐	☐	☐
/tʃ/	☐	☐	☐	☐	☐	☐	☐

1 Complétez chaque recommandation avec les voyelles manquantes.

a. T_RN _FF W_T_R b. R_C_CL_ P_P_R c. S_V_ _L_CTR_C_T_ d. R__S_ _W_R_N_SS e. PL_NT TR__S

2 Entourez le verbe qui convient.

a. You should (*have* / *sort*) your rubbish.
b. (*Reduce* / *Pollute*) waste.
c. People should (*collect* / *reduce*) rain water and (*sort* / *use*) natural energy.
d. Don't (*sort* / *have*) a bath but a shower.

3 Reliez chaque verbe à son synonyme.

a. implement •   • 1. diminish
b. reduce •   • 2. put into action
c. recycle •   • 3. separate
d. sort •   • 4. reuse
e. fix •   • 5. repair

4 Trouvez le mot correspondant à chaque définition.

a placard • pollutants • electricity • solar energy • rain • pollution

a. a large piece of card with a message on it, often carried in public to protest: ....
b. a form of energy that provides light, heat, etc.: ....
c. damage caused to water or air by harmful substances or waste: ....
d. energy that uses the power of the sun to produce electricity: ....
e. substances that pollute: ....
f. water falling from the sky: ....

5 Challenge!

Donnez le plus de conseils environnementaux possible en 1 minute.

6 Complétez les phrases avec *should* ou *shouldn't*.

a. We .... recycle rainwater.

b. People .... travel by plane but by train.

c. We .... use plastic anymore.

d. We .... reduce our waste.

e. You .... throw away* rubbish in nature.

f. We .... use reusable shopping bags.

**jeter*

7 Donnez 5 consignes à l'impératif en vous aidant des images.

....

....

....

....

....

8 Traduisez les slogans que vous voyez sur les pancartes.

....

....

....

....

9 Rédigez à votre tour des slogans pour la protection de l'environnement.

a. ....

b. ....

c. ....

TIPS

LANGUAGE

Exprimer un conseil : *should* + BV

À la forme affirmative

You should sort your trash.
Tu devrais trier tes déchets.

À la forme négative

You shouldn't eat too much meat.
Tu ne devrais pas manger trop de viande.

Exprimer un ordre ou une recommandation : l'impératif

À la forme affirmative : BV

Water plants with a watering can.
Arrosez vos plantes avec un arrosoir.

À la forme négative : do not/don't + BV

Don't have a bath but a shower.
Ne prenez pas de bain, mais une douche.

Word Page

AUDIO
foucherconnect.fr/23pttpm41

Nouns

a bath
un bain

a bike
un vélo

carbon emissions
les émissions carbones

climate change
le changement climatique

a dishwasher
un lave-vaisselle

electricity
l'électricité

an energy bill
une facture d'énergie

the environment
l'environnement

a means of transport
un moyen de transport

oxygen
l'oxygène

a placard
une pancarte

a plane
un avion

a pollutant
un polluant

a shower
une douche

a slogan
un slogan

solar power
l'énergie solaire

a tap
un robinet

waste/rubbish/trash
des déchets

a watering can
un arrosoir

wind power
l'énergie éolienne

Vocabulary

Verbs

clean *nettoyer*
collect *récupérer*
fix *réparer*
give* *donner*
implement *mettre en œuvre*
pollute *polluer*
protest *protester*
raise awareness *faire prendre conscience*
recycle *recycler*
reduce *réduire*
reuse *réutiliser*
save *économiser/sauver*
sort *trier*
start *commencer*
stop *arrêter*
turn on / turn off *allumer / éteindre*

UNIT 8

PROJECT

A2+

Create a poster

SCENARIO

À l'occasion de la Journée mondiale de l'environnement, votre classe organise une campagne pour la protection de la planète. Faites une affiche pour présenter un problème qui nuit à notre écosystème et proposer des solutions.

A2+

Faire des recherches sur un problème environnemental

- Choisissez un problème environnemental qui vous paraît important et sur lequel vous souhaitez sensibiliser votre entourage.
- Cherchez sur Internet des informations sur ce problème. Listez des solutions adaptées, des actions à réaliser, pour résoudre ce problème.

→ Environmental problem: ....
....

→ Actions

- ....
- ....
- ....
- ....
- ....
- ....
- ....
- ....
- ....
- ....
- ....

A2+

Réaliser une affiche

- Rédigez des phrases courtes à partir des informations listées précédemment.
- Exprimez des recommandations ou consignes avec la forme impérative et/ou le modal *should*, en particulier pour formuler vos solutions.
- Assurez-vous que les phrases soient claires et compréhensibles, sans erreurs d'orthographe ou de conjugaison.
- Insérez des illustrations, des photos, des dessins, etc. pour illustrer le problème choisi et les solutions. Vous pouvez également dessiner vous-même.
- Si vous avez choisi de faire une affiche à l'aide d'un ordinateur, agencez votre affiche de façon esthétique et lisible : choisissez une police d'écriture, mettez en gras, en couleur, soulignez ou encadrez certains mots importants...

MÉTHODE 4

Décrire une image

1 Observez le document.
- **Identifiez sa nature:** dites s'il s'agit d'une peinture, d'une BD, d'une affiche de film, d'une publicité, d'une photo, d'un dessin, etc. **(A)**
- **Identifiez son origine:** le titre, l'auteur, la date, la source ou l'endroit où l'on peut le voir (magazine, journal, BD, musée, télévision...).

2 Décrivez ce que vous voyez.
- **Précisez le lieu ou le décor:** un paysage, un portrait, une scène de la vie quotidienne.
- **Décrivez les éléments qui attirent l'attention:** objets, animaux, personnages. S'il s'agit de personnages: De qui s'agit-il? Comment sont-ils habillés? Ont-ils l'air joyeux, en colère, tristes...? Que sont-ils en train de faire? **(B)**

3 Observez l'arrière-plan, les détails.
Situez les objets et les personnages le plus précisément possible. **(C)**

4 Émettez des hypothèses.
S'il y a des personnages, imaginez les relations entre eux, leurs actions, le lieu... Utilisez les expressions adéquates. **(D)**

5 Donnez vos impressions et votre opinion sur le document.
- Dites si vous aimez ou pas le document et ce que vous ressentez en le regardant.
- Utilisez les expressions pour parler de ses goûts et exprimer ses sentiments. **(E)**

À retenir

AUDIO foucherconnect.fr/23pttpm49

A Identifier la nature
- an ad *une publicité*
- a cartoon *un dessin*
- a comic strip *une BD*
- a painting *une peinture*
- a poster *une affiche*

B Décrire les personnages
- He/She is wearing... *Il/Elle porte...*
- They look + adjective *Ils/Elles ont l'air + adjectif*

C Situer sur une image
- in the background *à l'arrière plan*
- in the foreground *au premier plan*
- at the top *en haut*
- at the bottom *en bas*
- on the left *à gauche*
- on the right *à droite*
- in the top left right hand corner *en haut au coin à gauche*
- in the centre/middle *au centre/milieu*
- behind/between/next to *derrière/entre/à côté de*

D Émettre des hypothèses
- Maybe *Peut-être que*
- We can imagine/suppose *On peut imaginer/supposer*

E Exprimer des sentiments
- What I like/don't like is that... *Ce que j'aime/je n'aime pas c'est que...*
- It reminds me of... *Cela me rappelle...*
- I find this document amusing/shocking... *Je trouve ce document amusant/choquant...*
- It makes me feel happy/sad/excited. *Cela me rend heureux/triste/enthousiaste.*

Écoutez attentivement les expressions ci-dessus et entraînez-vous à les répéter. Puis essayer de mémoriser au moins huit expressions que vous utiliserez page 86.

Entraînez-vous !

Donghai Liu, *"Phone Wall"*
Ad campaign, 2015.

1 Complétez la phrase suivante en vous aidant des informations autour du document.

This document is an .... entitled .... created in .... by ....

2 Observez le document et dites si les affirmations suivantes sont vraies ou fausses. Corrigez si nécessaire.

a. The scene takes place in a bedroom. ☐ Vrai ☐ Faux ....

b. We can see two people: a young man, maybe the father, and a little girl. ☐ Vrai ☐ Faux ....

c. They are sitting on a sofa. ☐ Vrai ☐ Faux ....

d. The little girl is playing with her mother. ☐ Vrai ☐ Faux ....

e. The mother is eating a piece of cake and reading a book ☐ Vrai ☐ Faux ....

f. The little girl looks very happy. ☐ Vrai ☐ Faux ....

g. The mother is ignoring her daughter. ☐ Vrai ☐ Faux ....

h. She looks glued to her computer. ☐ Vrai ☐ Faux ....

3 Complétez avec les mots suivants :

between • on the right • in the middle of • in the background • on the left

a. There is a beige sofa .... of the room.

b. The little girl is sitting ....

c. We can see a giant smartphone .... the little girl and her mother.

d. There is a chest of drawers* .... of the picture.

e. ...., behind a white lamp, there is a plant.

* *une commode*

4 Exprimez votre point de vue et vos sentiments sur le document.

....

5 Présentez une image de votre choix à la classe en suivant la méthode de la page 85.

UNIT 9 Films and Series to Watch (...or not!)

PROJECT A2+

Post a review of a TV series or a movie.

I RECOMMEND YOU TO WATCH

NETFLIX

SERIES	FILMS

A

Emily in Paris

Genres:
- ....
- ....
- ....

B

Sing 2

Genres:
- ....
- ....

C

The Witcher

Genres:
- ....
- ....
- ....

D

Resident Evil

Genres:
- ....
- ....
- ....

1 **Look at the document and describe what you see.**

2 67 **Listen and fill in the labels with the genres.**

action • adventure • animated • comedy • drama • fantasy • horror • musical • romantic • science fiction

3 **Tick True or False. Justify orally when it's false.**

a. *Emily in Paris* is a romantic movie. ☐ True ☐ False
b. *Sing 2* is a musical film. ☐ True ☐ False
c. *The Witcher* is a much appreciated TV series. ☐ True ☐ False
d. *Resident Evil* is a movie that is not very much appreciated. ☐ True ☐ False

UNIT 9

Popcorn movies

ACTIVITY A

A spectacular movie

Review: *Dune* Leaving Fans With Mixed Feelings

Dune, a new science fiction movie directed by Denis Villeneuve, is based on the 1965 *Dune* book, written by Frank Herbert. The film takes place in the year 10191 and is about Paul Atreides (Timothee Chalamet), who has to travel to the most dangerous planet in the universe to help his family. [...]

It's an intense and tedious film at some points. I found some parts of the movie lacking, such as the dialogue [...]. The movie was too long. [...]

Visually, this film was outstanding. The fight scenes were incredible, and [the special effects were] fantastic and visually impressive. [...]. The cinematography, costumes, and sets were all beautiful.

Coretta Wilkinson, veniceoarsman.com, November 19, 2021.

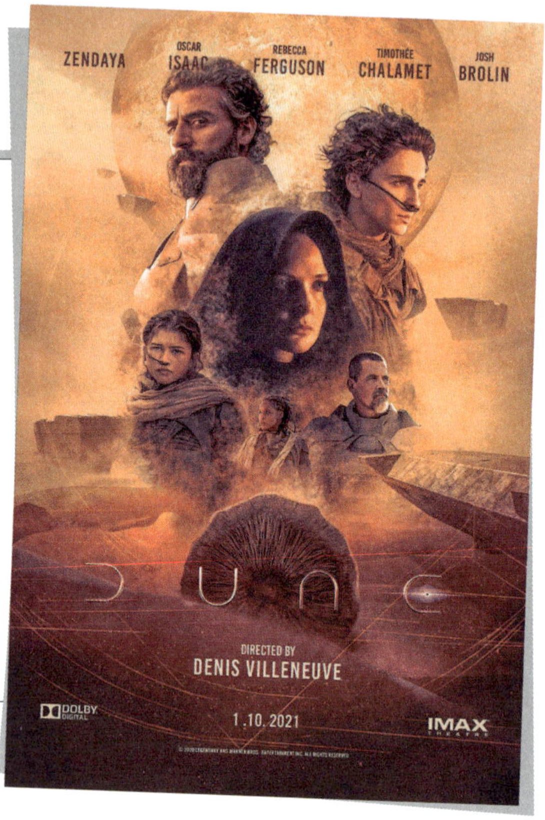

1 Look at the movie poster and complete the sentences.

a. The title of the movie is ....

b. The director is ....

c. The movie was released on ....

d. The actors are ....
....
....

2 Read the text above and tick the right answers.

a. The text is: ☐ a biography ☐ a postcard ☐ a review

b. The story takes place in the: ☐ past ☐ present ☐ future

c. The main character is: ☐ Paul Atreides ☐ Timothee Chalamet ☐ Frank Herbert

3 Find the English for:

a. *critique* (title): ....

b. *sentiments partagés* (title): ....

c. *ennuyeux* (§2): ....

d. *insuffisant* (§2): ....

e. *extraordinaire* (§3): ....

f. *impressionnant* (§3): ....

4 Find the adjectives corresponding to each aspect of the film. Circle the positive ones.

a. the dialogue: ....

b. the movie: ....
....

c. the fight scenes: ....

d. the special effects: ....
....

e. the costumes and the sets: ....

ACTION 1

Présenter les informations principales d'un film A2

Work in pairs. Choose one of the posters on p. 123 and present the film to your classmate. Then swap roles. You can fill in the table to help.

Streaming time

ACTIVITY B So many TV series!

1 [68] **Jessica watched three TV series last month. Listen to her reviews and fill in the information about the genre and the story.**

2 **Write the adjectives expressing Jessica's opinion.**

incredible • funny • amazing • boring • long • bad • amusing

3 [68] **Listen again and say if Jessica recommends each series or not, and why.**

a. *Vikings*: ....

....

....

b. *Ted Lasso*: ....

....

....

c. *This is Us*: ....

....

....

Genre	....
Story	The story is about ....
Opinion	– .... – ....

Genre	....
Story	The story is about .... hired to coach an English soccer team.
Opinion	.... /..............................

Genre	....
Story	The story is about .... that goes through many ....
Opinion	– .... – .... – ....

GRAMMAR SPOT

a. **The movie was too long.** b. **I highly recommend it.**

➔ *Soulignez les adverbes dans les phrases **a** et **b**.*

➔ *On place l'adverbe :* ☐ *avant* ☐ *après l'adjectif ou le verbe pour modifier son sens.*

Training ex. 7 & 8 p. 92

ACTION 2

Rédiger une brève description d'une série TV

A2

Use Jessica's notes below to write a paragraph to describe another TV series she watched: *Stranger Things*.

- **Genres:** science fiction / horror
- **Story:** secret experiments and supernatural forces
- **Positive Elements:** good actors / amazing special effects / fantastic music / really scary
- **Recommendation:** yes

UNIT 9

ACTIVITY C

In my opinion...

An intense conversation

●●●●○ Tip Top 4G 3:39 PM 75%

< Messages **Gwen** Details

So, did you watch Jurassic World last night?

I did and... I liked it!

Really?! Didn't you think it was tedious?

Tedious? Absolutely not! I thought the special effects were outstanding.

OK, I agree. I loved the special effects which were amazing but the story was BORING. And what about the actors?

Well, I believe the story was interesting and I honestly liked the actor who played the role of the dinosaur tamer.

We completely disagree! In my opinion, the actor was ridiculous!

We agree to disagree

iMessage Send

1 **Read the conversation between Gwen and Steven, and explain orally what they are about.**

2 **Find the English for:**

a. *Je pense:* ....

b. *Je suis d'accord:* ....

c. *Je crois:* ....

d. *On n'est pas du tout d'accord:* ....

e. *À mon avis:* ....

3 **Answer the questions.**

a. What film did Steven watch last night?

....

b. Did Steven like the film? Justify your answer.

....

....

c. Did Gwen like the movie? Justify your answer.

....

....

GRAMMAR SPOT

a. **I loved the special effects which were amazing.**

b. **I liked the actor who played the role of the dinosaur tamer.**

→ *Traduisez le pronom relatif encadré dans chaque phrase:* .... *et soulignez ses antécédents.*

→ *L'antécédent de «who» est:* ☐ *humain* ☐ *non humain*

→ *L'antécédent de «which» est:* ☐ *humain* ☐ *non humain*

Training ex. 6 p. 92

●●●●○ Tip Top 4G 9:48 PM 75%

< Messages **Gwen** Details

Hi! Did you watch the film scene? What did you think about it? Personally, I LOVED IT!

iMessage Send

....

....

....

....

....

....

....

....

....

....

....

....

ACTION 3

Répondre à un court message A2+

3:08

VIDÉO
The Niffler Scene – Bank Robbery

foucherconnect.fr/23pttpm11

Watch the scene from the movie *Fantastic Beasts* and answer Gwen's message by giving your opinion about it (special effects, actors, music, costumes, dialogues...).

UNIT 9

Training

AUDIO foucherconnect.fr/23pttpm12

in TUNE

A 70 **Écoutez et répétez les prononciations de la lettre « a » dans les mots suivants.**

/æ/ bad **/eɪ/** amazing **/ə/** adventure

B 71 **Classez les mots ci-dessous en fonction de la prononciation du « a ».**
Puis écoutez et vérifiez.

a. fantastic **b.** action **c.** agree **d.** animation **e.** appreciated **f.** musical **g.** character

/æ/	/eɪ/	/ə/
....	....	....

1 **Complétez le genre de ces films.**

a. A_ _ _ _ _ _ _ _ _

b. R_ _ _ _ _ _

c. H_ _ _ _ _ _ _ _ _
D_ _ _ _

d. H_ _ _ _ _

e. A_ _ _ _ _

2 **Reliez chaque adjectif à son synonyme.**

a. funny •	• **1.** incredible
b. boring •	• **2.** amusing
c. lacking •	• **3.** tedious
d. bad •	• **4.** missing
e. amazing •	• **5.** terrible

3 **Classez les adjectifs dans le tableau ci-dessous.**

funny • tedious • horrible • amazing • beautiful • amusing • bad • good • lacking • incredible • boring

Adjectifs positifs	Adjectifs négatifs
....	....
....	....

Challenge!

4 **Faites le plus de phrases possibles en utilisant les adjectifs de l'exercice 3 et les films ou/et séries TV que vous connaissez.**
Ex.: *Doctor Strange 2* is amazing.

Training

5 72 Écoutez et complétez les phrases avec les expressions manquantes.

a. ...., Zendaya is an amazing actress.

b. .... *Fast and Furious 9* was too long.

c. .... with most of the reviews. .... the story was bad.

d. The fans .... They .... the movie was outstanding.

6 Complétez les phrases avec *who* ou *which*.

a. I saw two friends .... were at the cinema yesterday.

b. Last night, I watched a Netflix movie .... was amazing.

c. In *Stranger Things*, there is a girl .... has supernatural powers.

d. *Batman* is a story about a rich man .... becomes a superhero.

e. *Titanic* is about a big boat .... hits an iceberg.

f. In *Star Wars*, Jedis have light sabres .... have various colours.

7 Réécrivez les phrases ci-dessous en ajoutant l'adverbe entre parenthèses.

a. Teenagers love scary movies. (really)

....

b. Nowadays, movies are long. (too)

....

c. People prefer watching movies at the cinema. (mostly)

....

d. Vikings were violent, like in the TV series. (pretty)

....

e. Fans criticized the last *Star Wars* movie. (strongly)

....

8 Remettez les mots dans le bon ordre.

a. currently / is / on Apple TV+ / *Ted Lasso* / available*

....

b. *Game of Thrones* / People / talked about / particularly

....

c. was / movie / This /violent / extremely

....

d. patiently / I / the new season / for / waited

....

e. interesting / surprisingly / was / *The Witcher*

....

**disponible*

TIPS — LANGUAGE

Les adverbes

On utilise un adverbe pour préciser la manière, le degré ou la fréquence d'une action.

En général, on peut nuancer le sens d'un adjectif ou d'un verbe en plaçant l'adverbe avant ces mots.

The special effects were visually impressive.
Les effets spéciaux étaient visuellement impressionnants.

I really liked this movie.
J'ai vraiment aimé ce film.

Les pronoms relatifs *who, which*

Le pronom relatif permet d'introduire une proposition subordonnée relative. Il représente et remplace son antécédent placé généralement devant lui.

Qui : *who* (humain)

It's about Paul Atreides, who has to travel to the most dangerous planet in the universe.
Cela parle de Paul Atreides qui doit aller sur la plus dangereuse planète de l'univers.

Qui : *which* (non humain)

This is a TV series which is too melodramatic.
C'est une série TV qui est trop mélodramatique.

Word Page

AUDIO
foucherconnect.fr/23pttpm10

Genres *Genres*

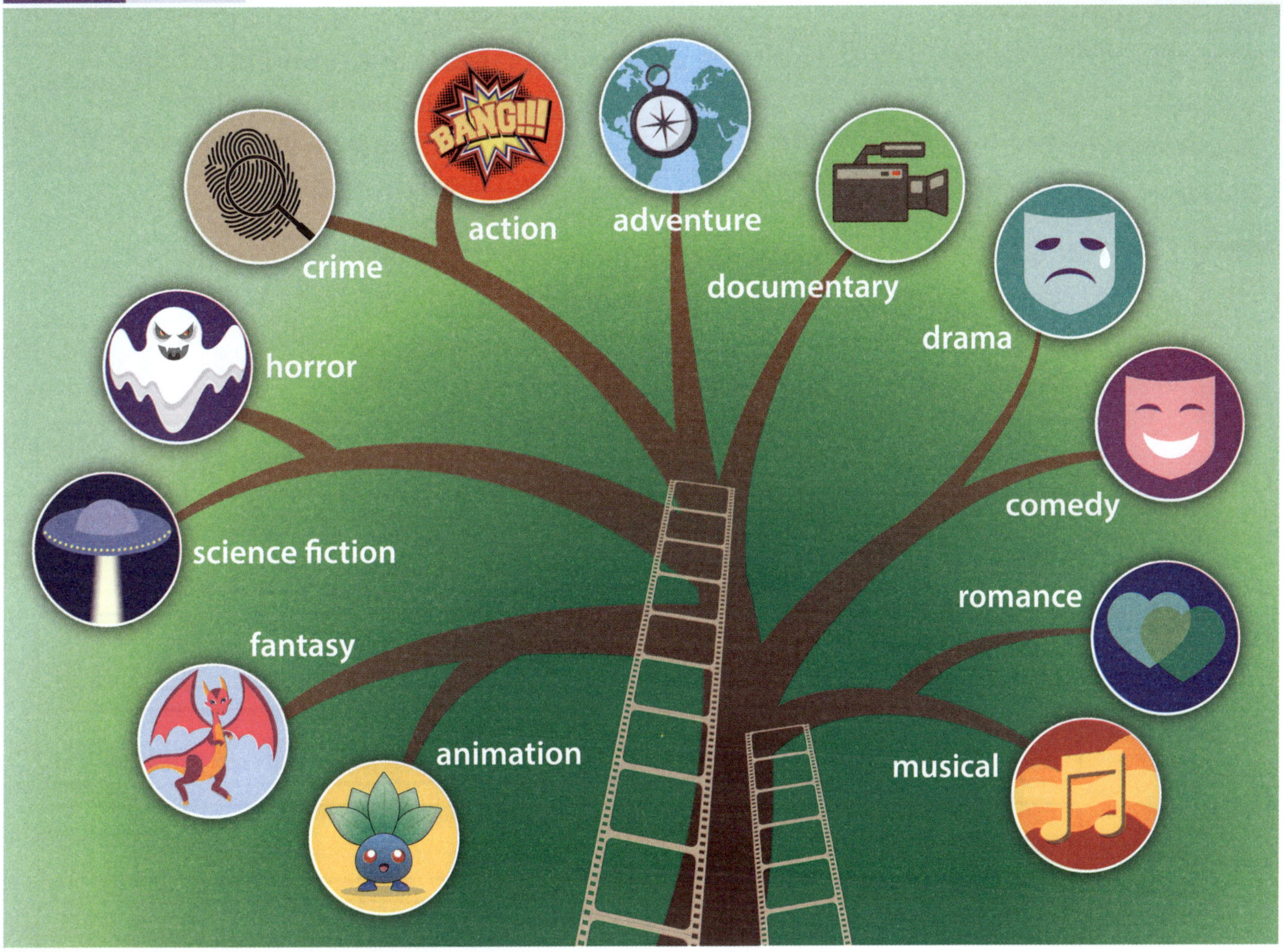

Vocabulary

Adjectives

+

amazing *extraordinaire*
amusing *amusant*
beautiful *beau*
fantastic *génial*
funny *drôle*
impressive *impressionnant*
incredible *incroyable*
intense *intense*
interesting *intéressant*
outstanding *exceptionnel*

–

bad *mauvais*
boring *ennuyeux*
lacking *insuffisant, qui manque de*
long *long*
ridiculous *ridicule*
tedious *ennuyeux*

Adverbs

absolutely *absolument*
also *également*
completely *complètement*
highly *extrêmement*
honestly *honnêtement*
personally *personnellement*
really *vraiment*
too *trop*
very *très*
visually *visuellement*

Opinion

I agree *je suis d'accord*
I believe *je crois*
I disagree *je ne suis pas d'accord*
In my opinion *à mon avis*
I think *je pense*

Elements of cinematography

an actor/actress *un acteur/une actrice*
a costume *un costume*
a fight scene *une scène de combat*
a set *un décor, un plateau de cinéma*
special effects *des effets spéciaux*
a story *une histoire, une intrigue*

UNIT 9

PROJECT

A2+

Post a review of a movie or a TV series

SCENARIO

Le site de votre lycée inaugure une rubrique critique de cinéma et séries TV en anglais. Mettez en ligne une courte présentation d'un film ou d'une série de votre choix ainsi que votre avis.

A2

Trouver les informations pertinentes pour présenter un film ou une série

- Choisissez un film ou une série que vous avez envie de présenter.
- Trouvez les informations utiles pour compléter la fiche ci-dessous.

→ Title: ....

→ Genre: ....

→ Director: ....

→ Main actors (2 or 3): ....

→ Release date: ....

→ Story: ....

....

....

....

→ Elements appreciated or not: ....

....

....

....

→ Your recommendation: ....

☆ ☆ ☆ ☆ ☆

A2+

Poster une présentation et un commentaire sur un film ou une série

- Créez votre article à l'aide de la fiche complétée ci-dessus. Rédigez des phrases complètes.
- Relisez bien votre article et mettez-le en ligne.

CULTURE CLICK 5 SHAKESPEARE'S MASTERPIECES

A

B

C

1 73 **Listen and fill in the grid.**

	A *Romeo and Juliet*	B *A Midsummer Night's Dream*	C *Macbeth*
Premiere* date	....	....	....
Main characters	.... and	Hermia, Demetrius and	.... and ....
Place	....	Athens	....
Genre	....	....	tragedy

* premiere: *une première/se produire pour la première fois (théâtre ou cinéma)*

2 74 **Complete the plots with the words from the list. Then listen and check.**

fairy • lovers • secret • witches • forest • hate • families • King • wife • magic

a. Three .... tell the Scottish general Macbeth that he will be .... of Scotland. Encouraged by his ...., Macbeth kills the king, becomes the new king, kills more people out of paranoia and ends up being killed.

b. Two couples (Lysander and Hermia / Demetrius and Helena) escape from Athens. In a ...., they meet Puck the .... who makes Lysander and Demetrius, the two boys, fall in love with Helena. In the end, Puck reverses the .... and the two couples reconcile and marry.

c. Romeo and Juliet fall in love at a party but they come from .... that .... each other. They marry in secret and plan to escape from their families. But a misunderstanding leads* the young .... to finally kill themselves.

* *un malentendu conduit*

QUIZ

1. Shakespeare was a playwright, a poet, and:
- ☐ a. a king
- ☐ b. an actor
- ☐ c. a singer

2. His nickname is:
- ☐ a. The Bard of Avon
- ☐ b. The English singer
- ☐ c. The King of London

3. He wrote about 38 plays and:
- ☐ a. 154 sonnets
- ☐ b. 1,540 sonnets
- ☐ c. 15,400 sonnets

4. In Old English, "thee" and "thou" mean:
- ☐ a. I
- ☐ b. You
- ☐ c. Me

5. His theatre was called:
- ☐ a. The London Theatre
- ☐ b. The River Theatre
- ☐ c. The Globe Theatre

6. In a movie adaptation, the role of Lady Macbeth was played by:
- ☐ a. Eva Green
- ☐ b. Audrey Tautou
- ☐ c. Marion Cotillard

7. Shakespeare's first play was:
- ☐ a. *Macbeth*
- ☐ b. *Henry VI*
- ☐ c. *Othello*

8. In *A Midsummer Night's Dream*, one of the characters has:
- ☐ a. a donkey's head
- ☐ b. a monkey's head
- ☐ c. a turkey's head

9. In a famous scene, Hamlet holds up:
- ☐ a. a skull
- ☐ b. a hat
- ☐ c. a cat

10. Shakespeare died on:
- ☐ a. April 23rd, 1616
- ☐ b. April 23rd, 1606
- ☐ c. April 23rd, 1564

76 **Listen and check.**

Your score: ..../10

VIDÉO 2:06
Mini Bio – Shakespeare
foucherconnect.fr/23pttpm30

3 Watch the video and answer the questions.

a. What was Shakespeare's first name? ....

b. Where and when was he born? ....

....

c. Who did he marry? ....

d. Who were the Lord Chamberlain's Men? ....

....

e. Name two masterpieces* written by Shakespeare:

....

* *chefs-d'œuvre*

4 Read this Shakespearean poem.

Shall I compare thee to a summer's day?
Thou art more lovely and more temperate.
Rough winds do shake the darling buds of May,
And summer's lease hath all too short a date.
Sometime too hot the eye of heaven shines,
And often in his gold complexion dimmed;
And every fair from fair sometime declines,
By chance, or nature's changing course, untrimmed;
But thy eternal summer shall not fade,
Nor lose possession of that fair thou ow'st,
Nor shall death brag thou wand'rest in his shade,
When in eternal lines to Time thou grow'st.
So long as men can breathe, or eye can see,
So long lives this, and this gives life to thee.

5 75 **Underline the right words. Listen and check.**

a. A sonnet is a poem with (*13* / *14*) lines.

b. In a Shakespearean sonnet, the (*first* / *last*) line rhymes with the third line.

c. The (*first* / *second*) line rhymes with the fourth line, and so on.

d. This set of four lines is called a (*quatrain* / *tercet*).

e. The last (*two* / *three*) lines are a couplet (a pair of rhyming lines).

6 Find the rhyming pairs in the poem:

1	day / May	5	.... /............
2	.... /............	6	.... /............
3	.... /............	7	.... /............
4	.... /............		

UNIT 10 The Stars Teens Love

PROJECT A2+

To discover famous stars or get to know them better, create a quiz about the personality of your choice and post it.

	Charli D'Amelio
.... →	**Charli D'Amelio**
.... →	2004
	Connecticut, USA
.... →	American
.... →	Social media personality – dancer
.... →	TikTok

	MrBeast
.... →	**MrBeast**
.... →	1998
	Kansas, USA
.... →	American
.... →	Social media personality – businessman
.... →	YouTube

1 **Fill in the document with:**

occupation • name • nationality • social media • born in

2 **Present the two personalities.**

3 77 **Listen and fill in the missing information.**

Charli D'Amelio	**Mr Beast**
Genre: dance	**Genre:** .... – gaming
Followers: ....million	**Subscribers:** ....million

© Éditions Foucher

UNIT 10

Promising stars

ACTIVITY A Millie Bobby Brown fans

1 (78) Listen and tick the correct answers.

a. Millie Bobby Brown was born in 2004 in: ☐ London, UK ☐ Marbella, Spain
b. She is: ☐ British ☐ Spanish
c. She is famous for playing: ☐ Eleven ☐ Nancy Wheeler in the series *Stranger Things*.
d. She started acting in: ☐ 2006 ☐ 2007
e. Since 2019, she has starred in: ☐ two ☐ four films.
f. She has also: ☐ started a beauty brand ☐ appeared in a lot of commercials

2 (78) Listen again and finish the questions.

a. .... was she born?
b. .... nationality is she?
c. .... is she famous for?
d. .... did she start acting?
e. .... films has she starred in?
f. .... has she become a millionaire?

ACTIVITY B A basketball prodigy

Victor Wembanyama

Born in a Paris suburb[1] in 2004, the French basketball player started playing when he was five years old. In 2019, he first played for Nanterre 92. And in 2022, he signed a contract with Metropolitans 92.

Wemby is very tall (2.20m) and he has become an extremely gifted[2] player. He has received two awards for best young player.

LeBron James said people have never seen anyone as tall as Wemby is. He also insisted on how "fluid and graceful" he was on the floor. NBA sportswriters[3] consider him to be "the most promising young player".

1 une banlieue 2 doué 3 journalistes sportifs

1 Read the article and complete the profile.

Name: ....
Nickname: ....
Born in: ....
Nationality: ....
Occupation: ....
Teams: ....
Awards: ....
Qualities: ....

2 Ask your partner three questions about the basketball player.

GRAMMAR SPOT

a. He <u>has received</u> two awards for best player.
b. People <u>have</u> never <u>seen</u> anyone as tall as Wemby is.
c. How many films <u>has</u> she <u>starred</u> in?

➜ *Le present perfect se construit avec :*
l'auxiliaire : ☐ have ☐ be +
☐ *la base verbale* ☐ *le participe passé du verbe*

➜ *L'ordre des mots à la forme interrogative est :*
(pronom interrogatif) + ... + ...
+ .... + *(complément)* + ?

➜ *Le present perfect s'emploie pour parler :*
☐ *d'une action future*
☐ *du résultat (présent) d'une action passée, d'un bilan*

Training ex. 7 & 8 p. 102

© Éditions Foucher

A short bio

ACTIVITY C Who is Ariana Grande?

1 79 **Fill in Ariana Grande's biography using the elements below. Then listen and check.**

famous • Florida • series • actress • equality • pop icon • voice • 15 • Positions

a. Ariana Grande is a singer, songwriter and ....

b. She was born in 1993 in ...., USA.

c. She started her music career at ...., but she gained fame when she played Cat in the TV .... *Victorious*. Since 2013, she has become a ....

d. Her four-octave .... is unanimously acclaimed.

e. She is .... for such hit songs as "Problem", "Bang-Bang", and "Thank U, Next". She released her sixth album, ..., in 2020. She has already sold over 85 million records!

f. She has also worked with many charitable organizations and fights for gender and racial ....

2 **Match the sentences above (a-f) and the titles below.**

Albums: ...... – Birth: ...... – Special talent: ...... – Occupation: ...... – Good causes: ...... – Career: ......

3 **Answer the questions.**

a. When did Ariana Grande become famous? ....

b. How many records has she already sold? ....

c. What are the good causes that she supports? ....

GRAMMAR SPOT

a. She started her career when she was 15.

b. Since 2013, she has become a pop icon.

Le temps employé dans la phrase a est le : ☐ *prétérit* ☐ present perfect

Le temps employé dans la phrase b est le : ☐ *prétérit* ☐ present perfect

Soulignez le mot qui signifie : « depuis ».

Ce mot est souvent suivi : ☐ *d'une durée* ☐ *d'une date*

Training ex. 6 & 9 p. 102

LET'S GO FURTHER!!!

INTERNET

foucherconnect.fr/23pttpm23

Read the first page of the information about the artist Shawn Mendes and recap in French what you have understood.

ACTION 1

Écrire une biographie

A2+

Use the information p. 125 to write a short biography of Drake or Beyoncé.

UNIT 10

Rich and famous

ACTIVITY D — A business magnate

1 (80) **Listen and tick the correct answers to the quiz.**

a. Elon Musk was born in South Africa in: ☐ 1965 ☐ 1971 ☐ 1977
b. When he was 17, he moved to: ☐ the UK ☐ Canada ☐ the USA
c. He is the CEO[1] of car company: ☐ Toyota ☐ Tesla ☐ Honda
d. He is also the CEO of aerospace company: ☐ SpaceX ☐ Boeing ☐ NASA
e. In 2022, he bought the social network Twitter for: ☐ $14 million ☐ $4 billion ☐ $44 billion
f. People have often criticized him for his opinions on technology and: ☐ art ☐ politics ☐ society

1 PDG

2 (80) **Listen again and write another item with one true answer and two false answers.**

Item: ....

☐ .... ☐ .... ☐ ....

ACTIVITY E — How to get media attention

Kim Kardashian was born on October 21, 1980. She is a very famous American media personality and businesswoman.

Kim and her family started acting in 2007 in a reality television series entitled *Keeping Up with the Kardashians.*

Kim's official website gets six million page views a month and she has over 10 million followers on Twitter.

Kim has created a fashion line with her sisters and she has also released a large variety of products: fitness DVDs, beauty products, a game app...

Critics have often described her as the person who wants to be famous for being famous.

When not working, Kim gives her time to charitable causes. She supports cancer research and fights for prison reform.

Underline in the article above the elements to answer the questions. Then orally answer each question.

a. Who is Kim Kardashian?
b. What is the title of the TV series in which she appears with her family?
c. How many followers does she have on Twitter?
d. What has she done to make money as a businesswoman?
e. How have critics described her?
f. What charitable causes does she support?

ACTION 2

Poser et répondre à des questions sur une personnalité (A2+)

Work in pairs. Use the documents p. 124 or 126 to ask and answer questions about Zendaya and Timothée Chalamet.

© Éditions Foucher

UNIT 10 # Training

AUDIO foucherconnect.fr/23pttpm14

in TUNE

A 81 **Écoutez et répétez ces mots comportant la diphtongue /ai/ ou /ei/.**

/ai/ icon **/ei/** fame

B 82 **Écoutez et cochez selon la prononciation. Puis répétez.**

	biography	space	play	gain	website	occupation	criticize
/ai/	☐	☐	☐	☐	☐	☐	☐
/ei/	☐	☐	☐	☐	☐	☐	☐

1 **Complétez les mots sous chaque image.**

a s___	an a_____	a r______	a c________	a s______ n_______

2 **Associez les métiers aux mots proposés.**

a. a singer •	• 1. lyrics
b. an actor •	• 2. a company
c. a businessman •	• 3. a ballet
d. a songwriter •	• 4. a record
e. a dancer •	• 5. a play

3 **Rayez l'intrus dans chaque liste de mots.**

a. VIP – celebrity – personality – contract – superstar
b. occupation – awards – equality – career – albums
c. singer – guitar – voice – politics – songs
d. team - writer – player – basketball – sport
e. company – CEO – game – dollars – business

4 83 **Écoutez et complétez.**

a. Kate Bush is an English singer, ..., record producer and ....
b. She was .... in 1958. In 2022, she became the oldest female .... ever to reach Number One in the UK charts.
c. She started playing the .... and composing songs at a young ....
d. She has released ten studio .... since 1978. She has won 16 ....
e. Her .... "Running Up That Hill" was used in season 4 of the .... *Stranger Things*.

Challenge!

5 **Choisissez une personnalité. Vous avez 2 minutes pour rédiger trois phrases qui devraient permettre à votre voisin de deviner de qui il s'agit.**

© Editions Foucher

Training

6 Entourez les verbes au prétérit et soulignez les verbes au *present perfect*.

a. Chance the Rapper released his mixtape *10 Day* in 2012.
b. He launched himself using SoundCloud and Spotify.
c. Since 2016, he has released only one studio album: *The Big Day*.
d. In 2021, he visited Ghana to meet Vic Mensa.
e. Since then, the two American rappers have frequently collaborated.

7 Mettez les verbes entre parenthèses au *present perfect*.

a. This businesswoman .... a new line of products. (*create*)
b. I .... already .... a Beyoncé concert. (*see*)
c. .... you .... a contract with a music producer? (*sign*)
d. This basketball player .... never .... in an NBA team. (*play*)
e. Since 2021, these two actors .... four film awards. (*win*)

8 Posez des questions au *present perfect* sur les éléments soulignés.

a. They have already produced <u>a TV series</u>.

....

b. Since 2010, the group has released <u>10</u> mixtapes.

....

c. <u>Elon Musk</u> has started some very famous companies.

....

d. This actress has become politically active <u>because she wants to defend gender equality</u>.

....

9 Répondez aux questions de façon personnelle.

Who is your favourite star? When did you start being a fan? Have you already sent them a message on a social media?

....

....

....

TIPS — LANGUAGE

Le *present perfect*

Il s'utilise pour exprimer le résultat (présent) d'une action passée et souvent pour faire un bilan.

Il se construit avec l'auxiliaire ***have*** au présent + **le participe passé du verbe.**

They have developed a new project. *Ils ont développé un nouveau projet.*

On utilise souvent le *present perfect* avec ***already*** (déjà) ou ***never*** (jamais).

Has she <u>already</u> starred in a series? *A-t-elle déjà joué dans une série ?*

He has <u>never</u> played football. *Il n'a jamais joué au football.*

Since (+ date ou point de départ de l'action).

We have won two awards <u>since</u> 2020. *Nous avons remporté deux prix depuis 2020.*

Present perfect ou prétérit

Contrairement au *present perfect*, le prétérit s'emploie pour une action passée, terminée et souvent datée.

Prétérit

She gained fame in 2005.
Elle a gagné en notoriété en 2005.

Present perfect

Since 2010, he has become an icon.
Depuis 2010, il est devenu une idole.

© Éditions Foucher

Word Page

AUDIO
foucherconnect.fr/23pttpm42

Life and Career *La vie et la carrière*

be born in
être né(e) en ... / à ...

move to ...
déménager à ...

start/begin* at (age)
commencer à (âge)

gain fame
gagner en célébrité

star in a film
jouer dans un film

sell* records
vendre des disques

sign a contract
signer un contrat

receive awards
recevoir des prix

release products
lancer des produits

become* a millionaire
devenir millionnaire

Celebrity occupations *Les professions de célébrités*

an actor/actress
un(e) acteur(trice)

a basketball player
un joueur de basket

a businessman/woman
un homme/une femme d'affaires

a CEO (Chief Executive Officer)
un(e) PDG

a dancer
un(e) danseur(seuse)

a producer
un(e) producteur(trice)

a singer
un(e) chanteur(teuse)

a songwriter
un(e) auteur(e) compositeur(trice)

Vocabulary

Nouns

a brand *une marque*
a commercial *une publicité*
equality *l'égalité*
a follower *un(e) abonné(e) (Internet)*
a game *un jeu*
gaming *des jeux vidéo, jeux d'argent*
a hit song *une chanson à succès*
an icon *une icône, une légende*
a record *un disque*
rights *des droits*
a sportswriter *un journaliste sportif*
a subscriber *un(e) abonné(e)*
a voice *une voix*

Verbs

acclaim *acclamer, admirer*
become* *devenir*
create *créer*
criticize *critiquer*
fight* for *se battre pour*

Adjectifs

charitable *charitable, caritatif(ive)*
famous *célèbre, connu(e)*
gifted *doué(e)*
graceful *gracieux(se), élégant(e)*
promising *prometteur(euse)*

© Éditions Foucher

UNIT 10

PROJECT

A2+

Create a quiz

about a personality

SCENARIO

Afin de faire découvrir les personnalités que vous aimez, vous créez un quiz sur la célébrité de votre choix que vous postez sur un site interactif.

Compléter une fiche biographique

A2+

- Choisissez une personnalité qui vous intéresse ou que vous appréciez.
  Vous pouvez choisir une personne célèbre issue du monde de la culture (musique, cinéma, arts graphiques...), des sports, de la politique ou de l'entreprise.
- Trouvez les informations utiles pour compléter la fiche ci-dessous.

→ Name: ....

→ Nationality:	→ Books, albums, films: ....
→ Date of birth:	....
→ Occupation:	....
→ Place of residence:	....
→ Famous for:	→ Awards: ....
....	....
....	....
....	....
→ Important events:	→ Other: ....
....	....
....	....
....	....

Réaliser un quiz sur une personnalité

A2+

- Utilisez les éléments de votre fiche biographique pour réaliser un quiz qui comportera 5 items sous forme de questions ou d'affirmations. Pour chaque item, vous proposerez 3 choix de réponses dont une seule sera la bonne (voir exemples A et B ci-dessous).
- Relisez soigneusement avant de déposer votre quiz sur un site interactif.
  Vous pouvez également créer votre quiz en ligne sur https://kahoot.com, par exemple.

Exemple A: Where was Elon Musk born?
- ☐ in the USA
- ☐ in Canada
- ☐ in South Africa

Exemple B: Wembanyama is:
- ☐ a dancer
- ☐ a rapper
- ☐ a basketball player

© Éditions Foucher

MÉTHODE 5

Répondre à un message écrit

1. **Identifiez la situation d'énonciation.** Qui écrit ? à qui ? Quelle est la forme du message : mail, post, lettre, carte postale, SMS… ?
2. **Lisez le message.** Repérez tout ce qui peut vous aider à bien le comprendre : les mots clefs, connus, et transparents.
3. **Préparez votre réponse :** écrivez vos idées au brouillon et organisez-les.
4. **Respectez les règles de grammaire.** Utilisez les temps appropriés.
5. **Utilisez des connecteurs logiques** pour structurer, complexifier ou hiérarchisez vos idées.
6. **Relisez-vous.** Prenez du temps pour corriger vos éventuelles erreurs.

À retenir

AUDIO
foucherconnect.fr/23pttpm50

A Exprimer son accord/désaccord	– I agree (with you). *Je suis d'accord (avec toi).* – You're right. *Tu as raison.* – I disagree (with you). *Je ne suis pas d'accord (avec toi).*
B Donner son opinion	– I think / I believe (that)… *Je pense / Je crois que…* – I don't think / believe (that)… *Je ne pense pas / Je ne crois pas que …* – In my opinion / To my mind… *À mon avis…*
C Connecteurs logiques	– That's why / That's the reason why… *C'est pourquoi / C'est la raison pour laquelle…* – Because *Parce que* – As / Since *Comme / Puisque* – For example *Par exemple* – First *Premièrement* – Secondly *Deuxièmement* – Then / Next *Ensuite* – To conclude *Pour conclure*

© Editions Foucher

Entraînez-vous !

Lila's phone

Messages Kirsty

Hi, I'm planning our New Year's Eve party. My parents will leave at 7 that evening so you can come after. Do you like watching movies? I was thinking we could watch one. Have you got any ideas? I don't know what we could have for dinner: pizzas? burgers? Let me know as my mum is doing the groceries next Friday, I can tell her what to buy. Talk to you soon.
XXO

Message

1 Lisez le SMS et répondez aux questions.

a. Qui envoie le message ? ....

b. Qui est le destinataire ? ....

c. Que prépare Kirsty ? ....

d. À partir de quelle heure Lila peut-elle arriver ? ....

....

e. Quelle activité Kirsty propose-t-elle ? ....

f. Que suggère-t-elle pour le repas ? ....

Kirsty's phone

Messages Lila

Hi! I can't wait to see you. My parents can drop me off at around 7:15.
I .... with you, watching a film would be great. ...., we could watch a sci-fi movie. ...., the latest Star Wars because it has great reviews. .... we could eat Pizzas and we could have a dance ....
I .... you are a fantastic dancer, you can teach me some moves. I will bring some sweets and sodas.
See you!

Message

2 Complétez la réponse de Lila avec les mots suivants.

agree • then • first • think • for example • party

My phone

Messages My best friend

Hi! How are you? Would you like to go shopping on Saturday? We could pick you up at 10. First, we could go shopping and then we could go to the cinema. I would love to see Timothée Chalamet's new film. He is a wonderful actor? do you agree?
Let me know.
XXO

Message

3 Answer your friend's text message.

....

....

....

....

....

© Éditions Foucher

EV@LANG

COMPRÉHENSION ÉCRITE

VERSION INTERACTIVE
foucherconnect.fr/23pttpm68

Reading – Part 1

Read the document and the question. Then choose the correct answer.

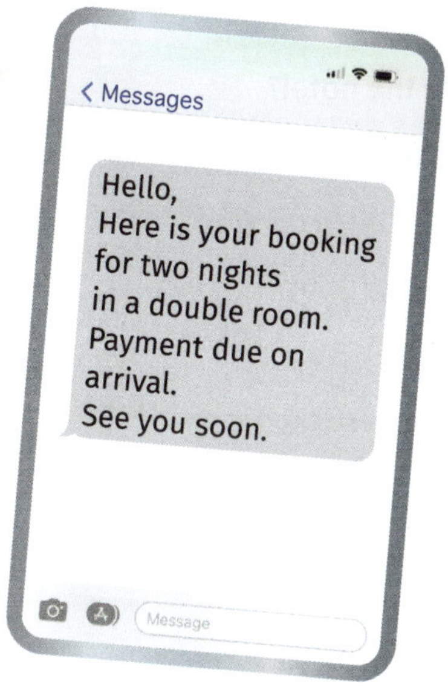

Who sent this message?

- ☐ A bank
- ☐ A shop
- ☐ A restaurant
- ☐ A hotel

https://myblog.com

Last weekend I went out with my friends to celebrate my birthday. It was sunny and we went to Hyde Park. We played softball. We rested and walked in the park. Then in the evening we went to the cinema to see an action film. Afterwards we had a pizza in an Italian restaurant. We ate and laughed a lot. My friends paid the bill because it was my birthday.

Reading – Part 2

Read the document and the question. Then choose the correct answer.

What is Tom talking about?

- ☐ His friends
- ☐ His holidays
- ☐ His favourite activities
- ☐ A perfect day he had with his friends

Reading – Part 3

Read the document and the question. Then choose the correct answer.

When the Cooper family went shopping, a young thief called Brian Fortune got into their house through an open window. He was looking for things to take when he heard their car come back. Brian escaped the way he had come in. While the police were looking for clues they heard the sound of a mobile phone coming from the garden. Detectives found the phone under some flowers where Brian had dropped it. It was his friend John who was still waiting for him outside. He didn't realise that he'd dropped his phone.

Who were the criminals involved in the burglary?

- ☐ Two brothers
- ☐ Two friends (one male and one female)
- ☐ The sons of the Green family
- ☐ Two friends (two males)

© Éditions Foucher

Reading – Part 4

Read the document and the question.
Then choose the correct answer.

Why is Ben writing to the hotel?

- ☐ To ask for a new suitcase
- ☐ To complain
- ☐ To offer an apology
- ☐ To book a room

Nettles Hotel
Park Road
Cardiff

CF 12 7GH

23 Carpenter's Lane
Rickwood
WD3 7HG

19th February N

Dear Sir or Madam,

I am writing to see if you can help me resolve a problem concerning a piece of luggage I took by mistake. I would also like to apologise for any inconvenience I have caused another guest at your hotel. When I got home last Sunday I discovered that I had accidentally taken the wrong suitcase.

I have an identical suitcase and picked the wrong one up without checking, leaving my own suitcase at the hotel. I am afraid that there is no label or other form of identification on the suitcase I took. Is there a way I can return it to its rightful owner and pick up my own missing luggage?

Once again, I'm sorry for what happened and any trouble it has caused.

Yours faithfully,

Ben Haynes

© Éditions Foucher

EV@LANG

COMPRÉHENSION DE L'ORAL

VERSION INTERACTIVE
foucherconnect.fr/23pttpm65

Listening – Part 1

Listen. Then choose the correct answer.

What nationality is Amy?

a. ☐
b. ☐
c. ☐
d. ☐

AUDIO foucherconnect.fr/23pttpm51

AUDIO foucherconnect.fr/23pttpm52

Listening – Part 2

Listen. Then choose the correct answer.

Where does the scene take place?

a. ☐
b. ☐
c. ☐
d. ☐

AUDIO foucherconnect.fr/23pttpm53

AUDIO foucherconnect.fr/23pttpm54

Listening – Part 3

Listen. Then choose the correct answer.

Where is the kitchen?

a. ☐
b. ☐
c. ☐
d. ☐

AUDIO foucherconnect.fr/23pttpm55

AUDIO foucherconnect.fr/23pttpm56

Listening – Part 4

Listen. Then choose the correct answer.

What is David taking to go to the beach?

a. ☐
b. ☐
c. ☐
d. ☐

AUDIO foucherconnect.fr/23pttpm57

AUDIO foucherconnect.fr/23pttpm58

© Éditions Foucher

Listening – Part 5

Listen. Then choose the correct answer.

How much is the tee-shirt David is buying?

- ☐ € 8.80
- ☐ € 8.90
- ☐ € 9.80
- ☐ € 9.90

AUDIO foucherconnect.fr/23pttpm59

AUDIO foucherconnect.fr/23pttpm60

Listening – Part 6

Listen. Then choose the correct answer.

What do we learn about Aileen?

- ☐ She gets on well with her brother.
- ☐ She wants to have her own home.
- ☐ She started a band with her friends.
- ☐ She works for a recording studio.

AUDIO foucherconnect.fr/23pttpm61

AUDIO foucherconnect.fr/23pttpm62

Listening – Part 7

Listen. Then choose the correct answer.

What is the advice for protecting the planet?

- ☐ to buy more products
- ☐ to use a reusable product several times
- ☐ to use a new single-use product every day
- ☐ to select eco-friendly materials

AUDIO foucherconnect.fr/23pttpm63

AUDIO foucherconnect.fr/23pttpm64

© Éditions Foucher

EV@LANG

GRAMMAIRE

VERSION INTERACTIVE
foucherconnect.fr/23pttpm66

Complete the sentences with the correct words.

1 His name is Paul. He ... 15 years old.
☐ am ☐ have ☐ has ☐ is

2 I don't like ... video games.
☐ play ☐ playing ☐ played ☐ plays

3 I ... born on December 15, 2008.
☐ am ☐ was ☐ have ☐ did

4 I ... in Watford, near London.
☐ 'm live ☐ living ☐ live ☐ lives

5 Where ... you from? – England.
☐ do ☐ are ☐ come ☐ is

6 What ... your job consist of?
☐ is ☐ are ☐ do ☐ does

7 ... is this dress? – It's £15.
☐ How much ☐ How many ☐ Who ☐ When

8 ... you repeat that, please?
☐ Do ☐ Could ☐ Must ☐ Are

9 Where ... you yesterday?
☐ did ☐ was ☐ were ☐ will

10 She usually ... a sandwich for lunch.
☐ eat ☐ eats ☐ don't eat ☐ have

11 Mark has a problem. Can you help ...?
☐ her ☐ him ☐ it ☐ them

12 Mary is just a baby. She ... walk.
☐ must ☐ mustn't ☐ can ☐ can't

13 ... you often play tennis?
☐ Do ☐ Does ☐ Is ☐ Are

14 London is ... than Paris.
☐ big ☐ bigger ☐ more big ☐ more bigger

15 ... bag is it? – It's mine.
☐ What ☐ Which ☐ Whose ☐ Where

16 How long have you been a painter? – ... 2015.
☐ For ☐ Since ☐ In ☐ From

17 Last week, I ... to the cinema with my brother.
☐ go ☐ went ☐ have gone ☐ been

© Editions Foucher

EV@LANG

18 **This is our apartment. It belongs to ...**

- ☐ us ☐ our ☐ my ☐ mine

19 **Tomorrow, if we can, we ... shopping.**

- ☐ will go ☐ go ☐ would go ☐ are going

20 **What time ... you arrive yesterday?**

- ☐ do ☐ are ☐ did ☐ will

21 **He is the actor ... plays in my favourite film.**

- ☐ whom ☐ which ☐ who ☐ how

22 **... tall are you? – I'm 1.70m.**

- ☐ How ☐ What ☐ Where ☐ How much

23 **This is the best film I have ... seen in my life.**

- ☐ ever ☐ already ☐ never ☐ always

24 **When did it happen? – Two months ...**

- ☐ last ☐ next ☐ now ☐ ago

25 **You won't succeed ... you work hard.**

- ☐ because ☐ unless ☐ but ☐ whereas

26 **The cheetah is ... animal in the world.**

- ☐ fastest ☐ the fastest ☐ the most fast ☐ the most fastest

27 **You ... obey the law if you don't want to be in trouble.**

- ☐ can ☐ can't ☐ must ☐ mustn't

28 **Look at these people! They ... in the street! Incredible!**

- ☐ dance ☐ danced ☐ are dancing ☐ are danced

29 **Stop ..., please! I have a headache.**

- ☐ sing ☐ to sing ☐ singing ☐ to singing

30 **If I were rich, I ... another car.**

- ☐ buy ☐ will buy ☐ bought ☐ would buy

31 **Would you like ... biscuits with your tea?**

- ☐ some ☐ any ☐ no ☐ a little

32 **He told me ...**

- ☐ to moving ☐ not moving ☐ don't move ☐ not to move

33 **We ... TV when they arrived.**

- ☐ watched ☐ were watching ☐ are watching ☐ watch

34 **It's your birthday. ... go to a restaurant!**

- ☐ Why don't ☐ What about ☐ Let's ☐ How about

35 **The walls ... with posters.**

- ☐ is covered ☐ are covered ☐ cover ☐ covered

© Éditions Foucher

EV@LANG

LEXIQUE

VERSION INTERACTIVE
foucherconnect.fr/23pttpm67

Complete the sentences with the correct words.

1 I work in a supermarket. I am a ...
☐ plumber ☐ gardener ☐ nurse ☐ cashier

2 In a bakery, you can buy cakes, sandwiches and of course ...
☐ meat ☐ bread ☐ vegetables ☐ fruit

3 This shop is open ... 10 am to 6 pm.
☐ to ☐ in ☐ from ☐ at

4 I need to drink. I am so ...!
☐ hungry ☐ thirsty ☐ tired ☐ sleepy

5 Can you ... your name, please? – Yes, of course. It's M.U.N.C.H.
☐ spend ☐ step ☐ spell ☐ stand

6 What time will you arrive? – At ...
☐ one hundred ☐ fifteenth ☐ twelve thirty ☐ o'clock

7 They ... go to school by bus.
☐ today ☐ always ☐ much ☐ very

8 This T-shirt is $120. It is ... expensive!
☐ too ☐ many ☐ lots of ☐ few

9 You can walk to the dentist's. It is not ...
☐ far ☐ near ☐ next to ☐ easy

10 This is my parents' house. And this is ... car.
☐ there ☐ they're ☐ their ☐ they

11 The concert is free, you don't need your ...
☐ wallet ☐ scarf ☐ bike ☐ watch

12 Would you like to come with me to the swimming pool? – Sorry, I'm ...
☐ happy ☐ fifteen ☐ excited ☐ tired

13 Your bedroom is a mess. You should ... it up.
☐ tidy ☐ see ☐ look ☐ fix

14 I would like to live in the South. It is not sunny ... here.
☐ quite ☐ enough ☐ rather ☐ also

15 He's going to work ... today. He will not be home before dinner.
☐ difficult ☐ early ☐ late ☐ at home

16 I hate sports cars because I don't like ...
☐ fast ☐ speed ☐ quick ☐ slow

17 My sister is really funny. She always makes me ...
☐ sad ☐ cry ☐ laugh ☐ angry

© Éditions Foucher

18 Goodbye everybody, I ... you a good weekend.
☐ wish ☐ want ☐ would like ☐ hope

19 John always has good marks. He is very ...
☐ stupid ☐ clever ☐ boring ☐ shy

20 "Geography" is a ...
☐ sentence ☐ summary ☐ quotation ☐ word

21 We won't go to the party ... the very bad weather.
☐ but ☐ despite ☐ unless ☐ because of

22 You had a very long day, you really ... tired.
☐ look at ☐ look ☐ look for ☐ look after

23 Having a shower is more ... than having a bath.
☐ ecology ☐ ecologic ☐ ecological ☐ ecologically

24 You have too many clothes! Your ... are full!
☐ cupboards ☐ placards ☐ sinks ☐ couches

25 This text ... feminism.
☐ speaks ☐ talks ☐ deals with ☐ about

26 My sister likes reading ...
☐ novels ☐ drawings ☐ movies ☐ characters

27 Use a ... if you want to remove the mistakes you made while writing.
☐ rubber ☐ ruler ☐ pencil ☐ highlighter

28 She's wearing sunglasses, I can't see her ...
☐ cheeks ☐ eyes ☐ lips ☐ chin

29 Flowers generally start blooming in ...
☐ spring ☐ summer ☐ fall ☐ winter

30 Last Christmas we ate ...
☐ a turkey ☐ a snowman ☐ garlands ☐ presents

31 He likes animals, he would like to become a ...
☐ butcher ☐ waiter ☐ vet ☐ hairdresser

32 They will be happy if they ... this match.
☐ win ☐ lose ☐ cheat ☐ earn

33 ... the light if you want to read. It's dark here.
☐ Cut ☐ Switch on ☐ Open ☐ Put

34 To protect the environment, plastic bags are ... in some countries.
☐ produced ☐ banned ☐ used ☐ designed

35 The trial was dismissed for lack of ...
☐ evidence ☐ jail ☐ charge ☐ convict

© Éditions Foucher

UNIT 1 Annexes

ACTION 1

p. 8

Student A

Personality 1 (woman)

Nationality	Swedish
Age	Born in 2003
Place of living	Stockholm (Sweden)
Occupation	Environmental activist
Family	1 sister
Pets	2 dogs

→ Name: Greta Thunberg

Personality 2 (man)

Nationality	Portuguese
Age	Born in 1985
Place of living	Madeira Island (Portugal) or Manchester (UK)
Occupation	Professional footballer
Family	1 brother and 2 sisters; 6 children
Pets	2 dogs and 1 cat

→ Name: Cristiano Ronaldo

UNIT 4 Annexes

ACTION 2

p. 39

Describe one of these rooms.

© Éditions Foucher

UNIT 2 Annexes

ACTION 1 p. 18

Student A

Use the document below to answer Student B's questions about your job as a waiter or waitress. Then ask Student B questions and fill in the information about his/her job.

Your job
Job: Waiter / waitress
Place of work: Restaurant
Tasks: take orders, advise and serve customers at table, keep the restaurant clean
♥: serving good food / seeing people smile and enjoy themselves

Student B's Job
Job: ....
Place of work: ....
Tasks: ....
♥: ....

UNIT 6 Annexes

ACTION 1 p. 58

Student A

KOBE BRYANT
Nationality: American
Sport: basketball
Team: Los Angeles Lakers
Nickname: Black Mamba
Skills[1]**:** dribbling, passing and shooting

1 *compétences*

© Éditions Foucher

ACTION 1 p. 38

Student A

PLAN A

Describe the house to your partner so that (s)he can complete her/his empty plan. Start your description with the children's bedroom because it is the only room that is marked on your partner's plan.

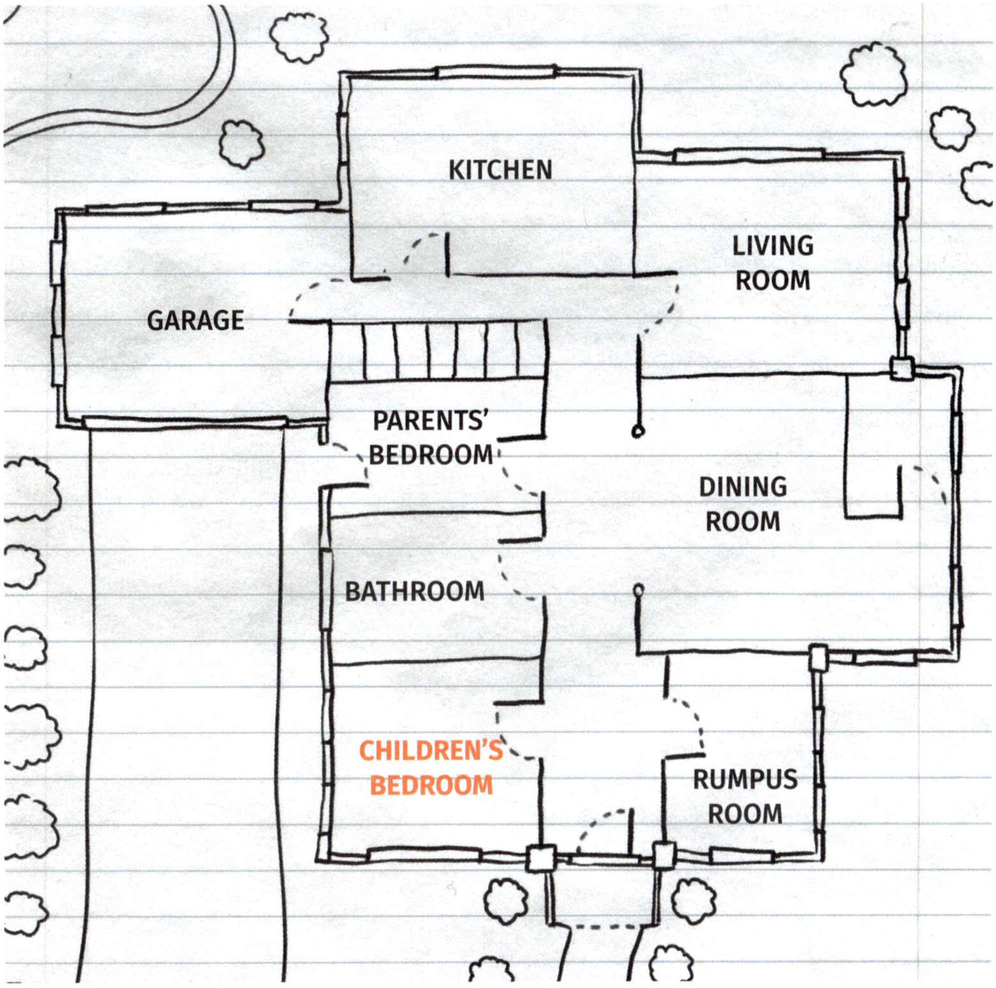

PLAN B

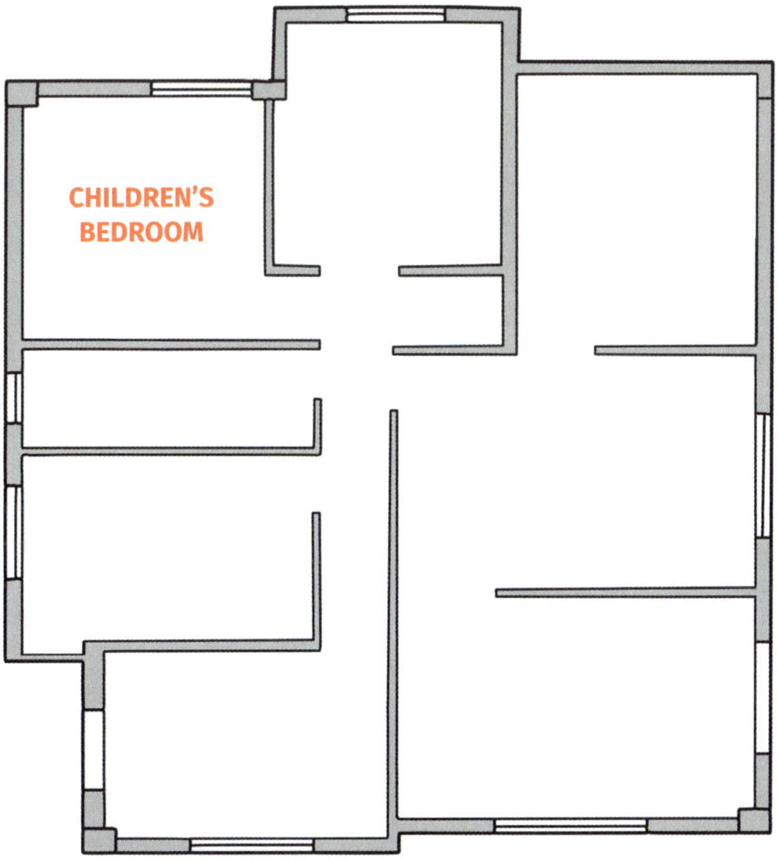

© Editions Foucher

UNIT 1 Annexes

ACTION 1 p. 8

Student B

Personality 3 (man)

Nationality	American
Age	Born in 1991
Place of living	Los Angeles (USA)
Occupation	Rapper, singer, songwriter
Family	1 brother and 1 sister; 2 children
Pets	1 dog

→ Name: Travis Scott

Personality 4 (woman)

Nationality	American
Age	Born in 1981
Place of living	Florida (USA)
Occupation	Professional tennis player
Family	7 brothers and sisters; one child.
Pets	1 dog called Chip

→ Name: Serena Williams

UNIT 4 Annexes

ACTION 3 p. 40

Choose one of these places of accommodation and describe it.

© Éditions Foucher

UNIT 2
Annexes

ACTION 1 p. 18

Student B

Use the document below to ask Student A questions and fill in the information about his/her job. Then answer Student A's questions about your job as an electrician.

Student A's Job
Job: ....
Place of work: ....
Tasks: ....
♥: ....

Your job
Job: Electrician
Place of work: Industries, companies or people's homes
Tasks: install, maintain and repair electrical systems
♥: designing and installing the equipment / meeting many different people

UNIT 6
Annexes

ACTION 1 p. 58

Student B

RUGBY
Number of teams: 2
Number of players: 15
Object used to play: an oval ball
Place: a field
Aim of the game: put the ball down at the opposite end of the pitch

© Editions Foucher

UNIT 5 Annexes

ACTION 1 p. 48

Student A

a. Present the event to your partner orally.

Time: 8:30 pm
Price: £64

b. Listen to your partner and fill in the chart.

Event	....
Date	....
Time	....
Price	....
Place	....

UNIT 7 Annexes

ACTION 1 p. 68

Present one of the companies and the tasks done by the intern.

Company 1

Name	The London Painting Company	**Number of employees**	15
Location	London	**Working hours**	8 am to 6 pm
Tasks	clean walls, prepare tools, paint and clean the site.		

Company 2

Name	Dublin Estate Agency*	**Number of employees**	8
Location	Dublin	**Working hours**	9 am to 5 pm
Tasks	welcome clients, answer the telephone, file documents		

* *agence immobilière*

© Éditions Foucher

UNIT 5

Annexes

ACTION 2 p. 49

Use the elements to act dialogues with your partner.

Invitations

STUDENT A: QUESTIONS	STUDENT B: ANSWERS
1 →	(-)

2 →	(+)

STUDENT B: QUESTIONS	STUDENT A: ANSWERS
3 →	(+)

4 →	(-)

© Editions Foucher

ACTION 1 p. 38

Student B

PLAN B

Describe the house to your partner so that (s)he can complete her/his empty plan. Start your description with the children's bedroom because it is the only room that is marked on your partner's plan.

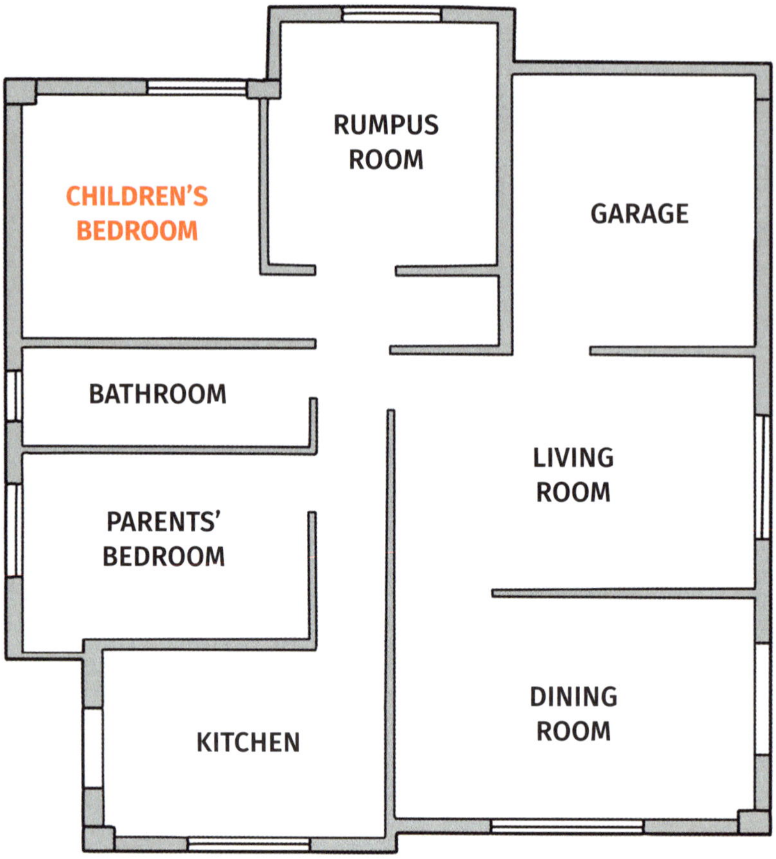

PLAN A

© Éditions Foucher

ACTION 1 p. 88

Choose one of these posters and present the film to your classmate. Then swap roles. You can fill in the table to help.

Title	....
Director	....
Actor(s)	....
Release date	....
Genre(s)	....
Period	....

© Éditions Foucher

ACTION 2 p. 100

Student B

Use the document below to ask Student A questions about Timothée Chalamet
Then answer Student A's questions about Zendaya.

Timothée Chalamet

Occupation:
....

Born:
....

Start:
....

Famous for:
....
....
....
....
....
....

Number of films:
....
....

Awards:
....
....

Zendaya

Occupation:
Actress – singer

Born:
September 1, 1996 in California (USA)

Start:
in 2010

Famous for:
- her role as Michelle in the film *Spiderman: Homecoming*
- her role as Rue Bennett in the TV series *Euphoria*
- her song "Replay"

Number of films, series, songs:
more than 12 films, 18 series, 10 songs

Awards:
33 awards and 86 nominations

© Éditions Foucher

Annexes

ACTION 1 p. 99

Choose one of the two artists and use the information to write a short biography.

BEYONCÉ	
Occupation	American singer, songwriter and actress
Born in...	September 4, 1981 Houston, Texas (USA)
Beginning of her career	start singing at 16 in an R&B girl group called Destiny's Child
Albums	sell over 250 million records (from 2003 to present) release in 2003: first solo album *Dangerously in Love*
Awards	win 24 Grammy Awards
Business	create a fashion line, a perfume

DRAKE	
Occupation	Canadian rapper singer, actor and businessman
Born in...	October 24, 1986 Toronto, Ontario (Canada)
Beginning of his career	act at 15 in the CTV series *Degrassi: the Next Generation* release in 2006: first mixtape *Room for Improvement*
Albums	sell over 170 million records (from 2010 to present) release in 2010: first album *Tell Me Later*
Awards	win 4 Grammy Awards + 6 American Music Awards
Business	found his own record label in 2012 create a fashion line

© Éditions Foucher

Annexes

ACTION 2 p. 100

Student A

Use the document below to answer Student B's questions about Thimotée Chalamet. Then ask Student B questions to fill in the information about Zendaya.

Timothée Chalamet
Occupation: actor
Born: December 27, 1995 in New York City (USA)
Start: in 2014
Famous for: – his role as Elio in the film *Call Me by Your Name* – his role as Paul Atreides in Dune
Number of films, series, songs: more than 20
Awards: 39 awards and 92 nominations

Zendaya
Occupation: ....
Born: ....
Start: ....
Famous for: ....
Number of films: ....
Awards: ....

© Éditions Foucher

ACTION 1 p. 48

Student B

a. Listen to your partner and fill in the chart.

Event	....
Date	....
Time	....
Price	....
Place	....

b. Present the event to your partner orally.

© Éditions Foucher

Crédits iconographiques

p. 7-mg .... ph © Rawpixel.com/Shutterstock
p. 8-2 .... ph © JUSTIN TALLIS / AFP
p. 15-1 .... ph © Disney XD via Getty Images
p. 16-hd .... ph © Pictorial Press Ltd / Alamy Banque D'Images
p. 16-b1 .... ph © Moviestore Collection Ltd / Alamy Banque D'Images
p. 16-b2 .... ph © Warner Bros. Television/The Hollywood Archive-File Reference # 34082
p. 16-b3 .... ph © Prod DB © Warner Bros. - DC Entertainment - Atlas Entertainment - Cruel & Unusual Films - Dune Entertainment / DR
p. 17-1 .... ph © Getty Images /fatihhoca
p. 27-2 .... ph © Image Source / Alamy Banque D'Images
p. 38 .... ph © With permission of Artist Iñaki © 20th Century Fox Film Corp, D.R
p. 35-1 .... ph © Queen Elizabeth II in March 2015/ Open Government Licence 3/Wikimedia Commons
p. 35-2 .... ph © Allan Warren - Own work/Duke of Edinburgh 33 Allan Warren.1992/CC BY-SA 3.0 /Wikimedia Commons
p. 35-3 .... ph © PRINCESS DIANA flag (5112486207)/Wikimedia/C C BY-SA 2.0
p. 35-4 .... ph © Prince Charles 2012/ CC BY-SA 2 /Wikimedia Commons
p. 35-5 .... ph © Camilla Parker Bowles - Duchess of Cornwall/Wikimedia Commons/CC BY-SA 4.0
p. 35-6 .... ph © 360b / Shutterstock
p. 35-7 .... ph © Featureflash photo Agency / Shutterstock
p. 35-8 .... ph © Prince Harry speaks during the opening ceremonies of the 2017 Invictus Games/Public Domain/Wikimedia Commons
p. 35-9 .... ph © FiledIMAGE/Shutterstock
p. 35-10 .... ph © Geoffrey Robinson / Alamy Banque D'Images
p. 35-11 .... ph © Anwar Hussein / Alamy Banque D'Images
p. 35-12 .... ph © Avpics /Alamy Banque D'Images
p. 35-13 .... ph © photo by Toby Melville/PA photos/ABACAPRESS.COM
p. 35-14 .... ph © Backgrid UK/ Bestimage
p. 36-3 .... ph © photoEdit / Alamy Banque D'Images
p. 39-d1 .... ph © Celebrity Big Brother: UK vs USA' TV show, Elstree Studios, Hertfordshire, Britain /Shutterstock
p. 39-d2 .... ph © Channel 4/Shutterstock
p. 39-d3 .... 'Celebrity Big Brother' TV show, Elstree Studios, Hertfordshire, Britain / Shutterstock
p. 39-b1&2 .... ph © photo by Scott Storey/CBS via Getty Images
p. 40-h .... ph © Graeme Peacock / Alamy Stock photo
p. 40-b1 .... ph © ITV/Shutterstock
p. 40-b2 .... ph © ITV/Shutterstock
p. 40-b3 .... ph © ITV/Shutterstock
p. 40-b4 .... ph © Joe Alblas/ITV/Shutterstock
p. 47-1 .... ph © Shutterstock/mozakim
p. 48-hg1 .... ph © ISTOCK/baona
p. 48-hg2 .... ph © ADOBE/Venture Studio
p. 48-hg3 .... ph © ADOBE/Diego
p. 48-hd1 .... ph © ADOBE/andrush
p. 48-hd2 .... ph © ADOBE/printstocker
p. 48-hd3 .... ph © ADOBE/Mockmenot
p. 48-b1 .... ph © Barry King / Alamy Banque D'Images
p. 48-b2 .... ph © Shutterstock
p. 50-b1 .... ph © ADOBE/Michael Mulkens
p. 55-hg .... ph © Genevieve Vallee / Alamy Banque D'Images
p. 55-m .... ph © ADOBE/Iryna Volina
p. 57-1 .... ph © Abbie Parr/AP/SIPA
p. 57-2 .... ph © GETTY IMAGES NORTH AMERICA / Getty Images via AFP
p. 57-3 .... ph © HANNAH PETERS / GETTY IMAGES ASIAPAC / Getty Images via AFP
p. 58-1 .... ph © BRUCE BENNETT / GETTY IMAGES ASIAPAC / Getty Images via AFP
p. 58-2 .... ph © PA Images / Alamy Banque D'Images/Paul Ellis
p. 60-1 .... ph © PCN photography / Alamy Banque D'Images
p. 62-2 .... Michael Reaves/Getty Images/AFP
p. 77-b1 .... ph © Rohan Chakravarty
p. 79-1 .... ph © SIPA USA/Alay Live News
p. 79-2 .... ph © Sipa USA / Alamy Banque D'Images
p. 82-b1 .... ph © photo by Paul Morigi/Getty Images for Green New Deal Network
p. 82-b3 .... ph © ADOBE/Ntabeleng
p. 82-b4 .... ph © Diptendu DUTTA / AFP
p. 86-1 .... © Phone Wall Campaign, Ogilvy Beijing, Client: Center for Psychological Research, Creative Directors: Shiyang He / Donghai Liu, 2015
p. 87-1 .... ph © COLLECTION CHRISTOPHEL © Netflix - Jax Media - MTV Studios
p. 87-2 .... ph © Collection Christophel © Dentsu / Universal pictures
p. 87-3 .... ph © Netflix / The Hollywood Archive /PictureLux /Alamy Banque D'Images
p. 87-4 .... ph © Collection Christophel © Constantin Film - Davis Film - Screen Gems - Sony Pictures Entertainment (SPE) - Tea Shop Productions - The Fyzz Facility
p. 88 .... ph © Warner Bros. Pictures / The Hollywood Archive/Alamy Banque D'Images
p. 89-1 .... ph © Collection Christophel © 2013 World 2000 Entertainment / Take 5 Productions / Shaw Media / Irish Film Board
p. 89-2 .... ph © COLLECTION CHRISTOPHEL © Apple TV - Ruby's Tuna - Universal Television - Doozer - Warner Bros. Television affiche americaine
p. 89-3 .... ph © COLLECTION CHRISTOPHEL © NBC - 20th Century Fox Television - Rhode Island Ave. Productions
p. 89-4 .... ph © COLLECTION CHRISTOPHEL © Netflix - 21 Laps Entertainment
p. 89-1 .... ph © BFA / Alamy Banque D'Images
p. 91-2 .... ph © movies / Alamy Banque D'Images
p. 91-3 .... ph © BFA / Alamy Banque D'Images
p. 91-4 .... ph © LANDMARK MEDIA / Alamy Banque D'Images
p. 91-5 .... ph © COLLECTION CHRISTOPHEL © Universal Pictures - One Race Films - Roth/Kirschenbaum Films - Perfect Storm Entertainment - Original Film
p. 95-1 .... ph © Romeo and Juliet By William Shakespeare, Publisher Wordsworth Editions, 15 Aug. 2022
p. 95-2 .... ph © A Midsummer Night's Dream: by William Shakespeare, Independently published", 17 Oct 2020
p. 95-3 .... ph © Macbeth by William Shakespeare, Publisher Collins, 2 Sept 2019
p. 97-1 .... ph © photo by Xavier Collin/Alamy Live New
p. 97-2 .... ph © photo by Vivien Killilea/Getty Images for TikTok
p. 98-1 .... ph © photo Credit: Netflix / The Hollywood Archive
p. 98-2 .... ph © Ethan Miller / GETTY IMAGES NORTH AMERICA / Getty Images via AFP
p. 99-1 .... ph © photo by Alexander Tamargo/WireImage/Getty Images
p. 100-1 .... ph © Ryan Lash / TED Conferences, LLC / AFP
p. 100-2 .... ph © Shutterstock
p. 102-1 .... ph © photo by Erika Goldring/FilmMagic/Getty Images
p. 115-1 .... ph © ITV/Shutterstock
p. 115-2 .... ph © Joe Alblas/ITV/Shutterstock
p. 115-3 .... ph © ITV/Shutterstock
p. 116-1 .... ph © Action Plus Sports Images / Alamy Banque D'Images
p. 120-1 .... ph © Barry King / Alamy Banque D'Images
p. 123-1 .... ph © Weinstein Company/courtesy Contributeur: Everett Collection Inc / Alamy Banque D'Images
p. 123-2 .... ph © COLLECTION CHRISTOPHEL © Warner Bros. - Bazmark Films - Roadshow Entertainment - The Jackal Group - Whalerock Industries biographie; biopic; biography; Elvis Presley affiche americaine
p. 124-1 .... ph © Fred Duval/Shutterstock
p. 124-2 .... ph © Shutterstock/DFree
p. 125-1 .... ph © Shutterstock/DFree
p. 125-2 .... ph © photo by Gabe Ginsberg/Getty Images

Autres crédits ..... stock.adobe.com

Paris – Mars 2023– 01 – NB-CB/VO

IMPRIM'VERT Votre imprimeur agit pour l'environnement

PAPIER À BASE DE FIBRES CERTIFIÉES

FOUCHER s'engage pour l'environnement en réduisant l'empreinte carbone de ses livres. Celle de cet exemplaire est de : 800 g éq. CO_2 Rendez-vous sur www.editions-foucher-durable.fr

Achevé d'imprimer en Italie par L.E.G.O. S.p.A. - Lavis (TN)
Dépôt légal n° 16842-2/02 - Mai 2024